S0-ADL-596

Guns, Violence, and Criminal Behavior

DATE DUE

HV
7436
.P65
2012

Guns, Violence, and Criminal Behavior

THE OFFENDER'S PERSPECTIVE

Mark R. Pogrebin
Paul B. Stretesky
N. Prabha Unnithan

LYNNE
RIENNER
PUBLISHERS

BOULDER
LONDON

KVCC KALAMAZOO VALLEY
COMMUNITY COLLEGE
LIBRARY

Dedicated to the memory of

Lyn Taylor
—MP

Albert Stretesky
—PS

Rajan Balachandra
—NPU

Published in the United States of America by
Lynne Rienner Publishers, Inc.
1800 30th Street, Boulder, Colorado 80301
www.rienner.com

and in the United Kingdom by
Lynne Rienner Publishers, Inc.
3 Henrietta Street, Covent Garden, London WC2E 8LU

© 2009 by Lynne Rienner Publishers, Inc. All rights reserved

Paperback edition published in 2012 by Lynne Rienner Publishers, Inc.

Library of Congress Cataloging-in-Publication Data
Guns, violence, and criminal behavior : the offender's perspective / Mark R. Pogrebin,
Paul B. Stretesky, N. Prabha Unnithan.
      p.   cm.
Includes bibliographical references and index.
ISBN 978-1-58826-665-1 (hc : alk. paper)
ISBN 978-1-58826-843-3 (pb : alk. paper)
1. Gun control—United States. 2. Violent crimes—United States. 3. Firearms
ownership—Government policy—United States. I. Stretesky, Paul. II. Unnithan,
N. Prabha, 1952– III. Title.
HV7436.P65 2009
363.330973—dc22

                                                                2009009889

British Cataloguing in Publication Data
A Cataloguing in Publication record for this book
is available from the British Library.

Printed and bound in the United States of America

The paper used in this publication meets the requirements
of the American National Standard for Permanence of
Paper for Printed Library Materials Z39.48-1992.

First paperback printing
Second hardcover printing

Contents

Tables and Figures

Tables

Figures

Foreword

THE UNITED STATES IS WELL KNOWN INTERNATIONALLY BOTH for high rates of homicide and for civilian gun ownership. Reasonably accurate estimates of the number of homicides and the number of firearms in US society are available and generally accepted by researchers and commentators. Yet, there is little consensus on the relationship between homicides and guns or on what policies are appropriate to address the problems that may be linked to widespread gun ownership. Although the public health perspective reminds us that firearms are a factor in suicides and accidental deaths, it is the belief that firearms make violent encounters in the United States more lethal than those in England and other similar societies that dominates scholarly, political, and public concerns. The 2008 Supreme Court decision striking down the District of Columbia's handgun ban, *District of Columbia v. Heller*, has ensured that policy debates will continue into the foreseeable future. And it is a given that thousands of US citizens will die from gunshot wounds each year.

Several types of data have been mustered by researchers representing the spectrum of current positions in the gun debate in attempts to increase understanding of the effects of firearms on violent crimes and to provide social scientific support for various policy alternatives. Cross-sectional analyses of violent crime rates and proxy measures of gun ownership have been a common approach, as have evaluation studies of legal interventions intended to influence who possesses guns and what they do with them. Grounded in the criminal events perspective, a recent flurry of studies has focused on how the presence of firearms, or firearms with particular characteristics (e.g., automatic firing mechanisms), affects the lethality of violent encounters. Although there are exceptions—beginning with James D. Wright and Peter H. Rossi's (1986) classic, *Armed and Considered Dangerous*—relatively few researchers have collected data from what is an essential source: the men and women who actually use firearms to commit violent crimes. The work of Lonnie Athens (1997) and monographs by Richard T. Wright and Scott H. Decker (1997) and Bruce Jacobs and Richard Wright (2006) are notable contributions to the slender, but growing, body of research that purposefully solicits the viewpoints of criminals on the role of firearms in crime.

This book by Mark R. Pogrebin, Paul B. Stretesky, and N. Prabha Unnithan joins the short list of studies noted above as a significant contribution to research that uses data obtained through interviews with criminals. Based on qualitative interviews with 73 inmates (67 men and 6 women) serving sentences for gun-related violent crimes in Colorado prisons, the authors analyze inmates' narratives of their past and projected experiences with guns.

The core of the study lies in two chapters on inmates' socialization experiences in reference to guns and an innovative analysis of their views on Colorado's recent "shall-issue" statute reported in a separate chapter. Pogrebin and colleagues find, not surprisingly, that street gang culture is the first milieu in which inmates sustain contact with firearms and begin attaching meanings to them. They find that the gun becomes a central part of the identity of gang members, and its connection to their willingness to do violence is an anchor for their sense of masculinity. Echoing Wright and Rossi (1986), they also report that a major instrumental function of guns is to avoid violence through intimidation of others. The authors' suggestion, supported by evidence from the interviews, that gun-related socialization continues in the prison environment—with many inmates gradually replacing their initial view of firearms as a means of protection to a symbol of power—is one of the most important findings in the book. Although there is some overlap, these different viewpoints on firearms have implications for policies designed to keep released felons away from firearms, and for how length of sentence served may impact recidivism among released inmates.

The authors make the interesting observation that criminals' beliefs and behaviors are rarely considered in debates over new legislation designed to reduce crime. Often, policy proposals are based on a conception of the criminal as a rational actor who makes a series of decisions, including sticking a gun in his or her belt or pocket when setting out to commit robbery or another predatory offense. This image is correct for some felons, but many are embedded in a street gang culture in which the risk of harm at the hands of others is a daily threat. For these men (and some women), carrying a firearm is a routine aspect of leaving the house or apartment apart from any plan to engage in crime. Their environment is dangerous, and the potential cost of being unarmed when trouble erupts often outweighs legal considerations.

Shall-issue laws that ease the restrictions on citizens' carrying concealed firearms are premised on a view of the criminal as a rational actor who will be deterred by the increased likelihood of encountering an armed victim or bystander when committing an offense. Pogrebin and colleagues' questioning of inmates on their views of the Colorado shall-issue law elicited a range of responses with policy implications. Some interviewees shared the dominant perspective that they would be less likely to commit an offense if they thought the intended victim was armed. Others indicated that they would escalate their use of violence, in some cases to the level of a preemptive strike, by shooting first and sorting out the details later. The overall effect of the law presumably would depend on the relative proportions of the two types of responses among motivated offenders, which are unknown. This finding should give pause to proponents of new legislation designed to reduce gun crimes who have not considered the likely range of responses by criminals. It also argues for a greater exchange of ideas and facts between policymakers and social scientists in the legislative process.

As a final note, some of the book's findings may be specific to Colorado or perhaps Colorado and a group of similar states. Being more familiar with the types of guns used in crimes and the illegal firearms markets in central Florida, I was surprised to learn that 50 percent of the guns used by the interviewees were revolvers, a type of firearm that is rare among crime guns in many locations. The prevalence of revolvers is undoubtedly related to the frontier tradition in Colorado, but the high representation of .25- and .38-caliber handguns is of more significance. These weapons are at the low end of the available weaponry on the streets in central Florida, where police are increasingly worried about the proliferation of assault rifles. Of course, the existence of regional differences in the use of firearms in crime is not a criticism of this study. Instead, it points to the need for replications to be completed in other states. The authors have provided future researchers with an excellent model to follow. Their work deserves widespread and close attention within criminological and policy circles.

—Jay Corzine
University of Central Florida

Preface

THERE ARE SIGNIFICANT COSTS AND BENEFITS TO LIVING IN A nation with around 218 million guns in circulation (Hepburn et al. 2007). According to the US Centers for Disease Control and Prevention, about 99,000 individuals received nonfatal wounds and nearly 38,000 died in one year from gunshots, with slightly less than half of these classified as homicides (Zavitz 1996). Some of those cases that were not classified as homicides were attributed to defensive gun use. Kleck and Gertz (1998) conclude that there are nearly 2.5 million instances a year where guns are used for defensive purposes. Yet, it is estimated that gun violence costs the United States $100 billion annually (Cook and Ludwig 2000).

The vast majority of research on gun use is quantitative in nature, focusing on summarizing why individuals own long guns and handguns and on assessing the net effect of widespread gun ownership on violence. In addition, there is a great deal of quantitative research that focuses on public opinion and attitudes about guns and on the positive and negative impact of gun laws and policies. The purpose of this book is to present readers with narrative accounts of violent gun use from the perspective of gun offenders. The methodological approach taken is naturalistic and allows violent gun offenders to discuss their offenses, lifestyles, and opinions from their own perspective. Giving voice to the offender provides a portrayal of gun use by those who have the direct experience of participating in violent gun offenses.

We draw from and expand upon research previously published in

Mark R. Pogrebin, Paul B. Stretesky, N. Prabha Unnithan, and Gerry Venor, "Retrospective Accounts of Violent Events by Gun Offenders," *Deviant Behavior* 27, no. 4 (2006): 479–501; Paul B. Stretesky and Mark R. Pogrebin, "Gang-Related Gun Violence: Socialization, Identity, and Self," *Journal of Contemporary Ethnography* 36, no. 1 (2007): 85–114; Paul B. Stretesky, Mark R. Pogrebin, N. Prabha Unnithan, and Gerry Venor, "Prisonization and Accounts of Gun Carrying," *Journal of Criminal Justice* 35, no. 5 (2007): 485–497; and N. Prabha Unnithan, Mark R. Pogrebin, Paul B. Stretesky, and Gerry Venor, "Gun Felons and Gun Regulation: Offenders' Views About and Reactions to 'Shall Issue' Policies for Carrying Concealed Weapons," *Criminal Justice Policy Review* 19, no. 2 (2008): 196–214. Specifically, we focus on accounts of gun violence: some of the factors that led up to the event (e.g., how gang socialization and culture influences perceptions regarding guns), if and how the offender's view of guns has changed after being convicted and punished through incarceration, and what he or she believes might happen in response to easier access to carrying concealed weapons.

Our goal is not to reframe the contentious debate on guns and their place in US society and politics (see Utter 2000; Wilson 2006). Instead, we hope that this work offers some insight into the minds of those individuals who use guns during a crime. We do this by asking offenders to reflect on their past, in terms of the violence and crime that they perpetrated, by (1) contemplating their present circumstances of incarceration and the time-related changes that have taken place, and (2) looking to the future as they imagine themselves in similar situations where the potential for violence may exist. The narratives constructed and presented by the incarcerated felons during the course of those extended conversations are the mainstay of the chapters that follow.

—*Mark R. Pogrebin,*
Paul B. Stretesky,
N. Prabha Unnithan

Acknowledgments

THIS BOOK IS THE CULMINATION OF A RESEARCH PROJECT ON the use of guns in the commission of violent crimes. The three of us, living in cities and teaching on campuses (Colorado State University at Fort Collins and the University of Colorado at Denver) located along Colorado's Front Range, have known each other professionally and personally for many years. However, we did not work together until we began this project. In the course of studying the topic, discussing and debating it during our trips to various prisons, and working on related publications, we have also become friends. We have melded our own intellectual interests, critiqued each other's ideas, and commingled our voices in the course of researching and writing the chapters that constitute this book. Therefore, the book is a joint effort in the best sense of the term: one to which all three of us, although we are listed alphabetically as coauthors, have contributed equally from its initial conceptualization to final execution.

Several people have aided us in formulating and completing the research underlying the book, in collecting data, and in writing it. We first acknowledge the assistance of Gerry Venor and Howard Eiden, who arranged for and conducted several interviews with inmates. We greatly appreciate the amount of time and effort that Gerry and Howard contributed to this project. We are indebted to former US attorney for the District of Colorado, John Suthers, who provided us with grant support through the Justice Department's Project Safe Neighborhoods program. We thank Richard Weatherby, also from the

US Attorney's Office, for his encouragement and support. We are appreciative of the Colorado Department of Corrections Office of Planning and Analysis manager, C. Scott Hromas, whose assistance was invaluable at the beginning of this research. We thank the staff at the various penitentiaries and are especially grateful for their help in providing us with space and time to carry out our work as we interviewed inmates.

We are grateful to Jay Corzine for kindly consenting to write the foreword to the book. For the past three decades, he has contributed immensely to the advancement of social scientific knowledge regarding various forms of violence ranging from lynching to homicide, and we are honored by his support of our efforts. Unnithan would also like to acknowledge Colorado State University for providing him with a sabbatical to support his work on this project.

All three of us thank our own families for their patience and forbearance while we traveled across the state to visit prisons in 2003 and 2004. Specifically, Pogrebin thanks and dedicates this book to his late wife, Lyn Taylor, who, through her love, continues to be a constant inspiration to him in his research and in his life, and to Russell Beaulieu, teacher, friend, and mentor in more ways than he will ever know. Stretesky thanks his wife, Christine, and their sons, Denver and Mason. They were very supportive and understanding during the interviews, coding of data, and various revisions to the manuscript. Christine has, once again, shouldered much of the burden of this research in the form of an unfair distribution of family labor. Unnithan thanks his wife, Shashikala, and their daughters, Rachna and Ranjana, all of whom have had to listen to more than their fair share of prison stories. On a more somber note, he dedicates this book to Rajan Balachandra, a favorite nephew, who died at the age of 29 in March 2003 in Kuala Lumpur, Malaysia, as a result of a tragic accident.

At Lynne Rienner Publishers, we have been fortunate to work with acquisitions editor Andrew Berzanskis, who remained supportive, encouraging, and enthusiastic from the time we proposed the idea for this book to him. Our reviewers, Dean Dabney (at Georgia State University) and Tom Kovandzic (at the University of Texas–Dallas), pushed us to rethink and revise particular sections of the book, and we are appreciative of their helpful comments.

Finally, and most importantly, we are grateful to the 73 Colorado inmates who responded to our call for participation in a research project that provided them with little by way of tangible benefits. They spent many hours patiently and candidly recounting for us their personal histories of involvement with guns, criminal behavior, and violence. We are not exaggerating when we say that, without them, this book could not and would not have been written.

1

Introduction:
The Gun Offender's
Perspective

ANY STUDY THAT SEEKS TO EXPLAIN GUN VIOLENCE MUST BEGIN by asking the why and how of the actual offense. We believe that the best way to approach the study of gun violence is to talk with offenders who have used a gun in the commission of a violent crime. *Guns, Violence, and Criminal Behavior: The Offender's Perspective* tells the stories of individuals who have used a firearm in the commission of a violent crime. The focus is on the offenders and their views on various subjects about guns generally and their own illegal use specifically. We explore important issues regarding multiple dimensions of gun-related violence based on first-hand narratives elicited from gun offenders who discuss those whys and hows. The offenders who speak throughout this book relate their experiences and perceptions about guns and the violent events that resulted in their incarceration. However, this book is not only about gun use during the commission of a violent crime. It is also about the offenders who were willing to be interviewed and tape-recorded for the study.

The Offender's Perspective

We believe that the best way to grasp the meaning and interpretation of the offender's violent crime is to ask inmates about their experiences with firearms and how they came to use guns to kill or injure

1

others. The stories told by the inmates in this book confront their own thoughts about guns and the use of guns in violent events. They share their views about gangs and firearms, the time of incarceration as it impacts opinions about various uses of firearms, and their ideas concerning the pros and cons of citizens being permitted to more easily carry concealed weapons. We collected all of the data as it was narrated to us by the offenders. We tape-recorded each offender's story so that we could examine his or her perceptions about guns, violence, and criminal behavior. As the interviews progressed, it became clear to us that there exists a method to what is often perceived as the madness of violent gun use. As inmates related their own stories, along with our probing on relevant issues, a pattern of attitudes and thoughts developed. Inmates often described the incidents that led up to their violent events as being determined by forces outside of their control. Many inmates claimed that they believe they had no other choice in the situation but to use their gun to harm, murder, or intimidate another person. In short, they constantly related their reconstruction of the events that caused them to feel that their use of the firearm was rational at the time. To them, it was the only possible choice they could have made at the moment.

What is striking about the majority of the criminological literature on gun offending is just how few studies are based methodologically on the perspectives and life stories of the gun users themselves. Large-scale survey research data on gun use have much to offer. However, even with the collection of data from a great number of respondents and the presentation of the results of sophisticated statistical analyses, it has not been possible to fully represent just who these violent gun offenders are; to directly assess the life histories that caused them to think about violent gun use the way that they do; or to adequately explain the series of decisions that led to violent, and sometimes deadly, outcomes.

This research, then, attempts to present new ideas about men and women who see the use of guns in the various circumstances of everyday life as reasonable. By looking at gun use through the eyes of those who have been found guilty of a violent gun-related offense, we give each inmate the opportunity to discuss issues that many law-abiding citizens in the community ask about them, but rarely receive answers to. Although the subject of gun use in the commission of a felony is a fascinating one, the people we interviewed (i.e., the actual perpetrators of such violent acts) are even more interesting to us as researchers. By discovering who these gun users are, it was possible for us to cut through the stereotypical definitions of such people. All of us in society at one time or another have asked the question: What kind of person would commit such a criminal act? We often think of such offending individuals as despicable and subhuman. We would never want to personally get to know a murderer and certainly never become acquainted informally with a person of that character. We think of violent gun offenders as individuals who are very different from ourselves, who reside in a community unlike ours, or who associate with a dissimilar and particularly loathsome social group. These offenders appear poles apart from the middle-class mainstream so that we can in no way relate to them. Yet as the interviews progressed, we began to realize that the inmates we spoke with actually are not that different from the rest of society. Let us explain.

We do not deny the amount of damage and the seriousness of the harm that these inmates have caused. We do not empathize with their acts that have destroyed lives, families, and communities. At the same time, we believe that most members of society would argue that they would never use a gun to harm others. This perception is understandable because those individuals who would utilize violent means for conflict resolution or for material gain (or both) are just plain frightening to most of us. But if it were possible to take away these inmates' prison garb and current state of incarceration and place them in the community, the majority of us would have a difficult time identifying them as criminals. Our false stereotypes of violent offenders (Swigert and Farrell 1977) and just who they are, what they look like, and how their acts portray them to us result in a false sense of the existence of physical and social differences. These differences allow us to go about our lives with the view that we could never indulge in or be impacted by such violence. This sense of difference prompted us to ask the interviewees several questions about violent gun use: Who are you and what is your background? Why do people use violent means to solve conflicting interpersonal disputes? What do you think about the use of guns and the numerous policy issues that surround the ease of acquiring guns and their widespread availability? We share their answers to these questions as well as their stories throughout this book.

This study of gun-offending persons was funded by the US Department of Justice's Project Safe Neighborhoods program, which had as its primary goal the elimination of illegal guns within the communities in our country. The granting agency, the US Attorney's Office in Colorado, was most interested in where illegal firearms were procured and how they were used to commit crimes. Although we were interested in the same questions, we felt it necessary to expand this research by probing about multiple issues in addition to those questions requested by the sponsoring agency. For us, the necessity to inquire about gun issues and social and criminal histories provided us with some insight into the lives of gun offenders before they committed their violent actions. Further, our approach of utilizing intensive semistructured interviewing provided the participants with an opportunity to relate their life story or event history retrospectively in some sequential order. In summary, by telling about their lives before incarceration, the interviewees were able to relate their life experiences in some logical and meaningful fashion and in a way that led them to the actual event or events that resulted in their current incarceration.

It certainly could be argued that retrospective accounts of an individual's prior criminal activities are a mixture of fact and fantasy, with damaging information withheld, particularly facts pertaining to the actual harm the offender may have done to the victim as a result of his or her violent behavior. We do not disagree with this argument, except to note that the embellished story that an inmate may tell is just as important to the research as the factual data. That is, we are and should be interested in accounts of events, even those that may have been manipulated retrospectively. At the same time, it should be noted that we had access to the official prison file of each inmate before we interviewed him or her. These files contained information such as prior probation reports, police reports, and criminal history. This permitted us to make a judgment concerning the veracity of the interviewee's recounting of events that led up to the current incarceration. In general, the majority of the interviewees related their past history, at least the criminal part, closely to the facts that we found in their prison file.

After meeting and interviewing the very people who have used firearms in their offenses, we as researchers came away from the experience with a different view of who these offenders are. In a small way, our hidden stereotypes of violent gun users also changed. Like everyone else, we had read newspaper reports and watched the nightly news, which subconsciously influenced our thoughts about these offenders. Thus, perhaps we were somewhat jaded in our perceptions of the study participants prior to the interviews. Suffice it to say that we also learned that a person does not have to be socialized into some form of criminal culture over a long period of time to end up in prison for using a firearm for criminal purposes. We need to point out at this particular juncture that major differences in the backgrounds of the gun offenders represented in this study are too numerous to justify such an assumption.

The foregoing discussion needs additional commentary that puts the stereotype of violent gun offenders in some perspective. That is, it is necessary for us to clarify just who the inmates we interviewed were. After spending considerable time interviewing the study population about the crime that led to their current conviction and imprisonment, together with their life and criminal histories, we came to the realization that not everyone who uses a firearm for the purposes of monetary gain or actually shoots another person for any reason is similar in nature. Although we found many similarities in patterns of thinking and perception among these gun offenders, we also found just as many differences. What we intend to make clear to readers, at this point, is the realization that the interviews revealed a number of gun offenders who were not steeped in a culture of crime, but who in fact were never involved in any criminal activity except for occasional recreational drug use. Thus, students of gun violence should understand the distinct differences that exist between what we term *novice* gun offenders and those who are more *experienced* and whose involvement in criminal activity in general is characterized by a long and violent history. For many, violence came neither easily nor automatically (Collins 2008). In a sense, it is safe to say that, ultimately, all of the interviewees had only one thing in common: very long sentences in Colorado prisons.

By way of example, we found a 19-year-old woman who shot and killed her boyfriend before shooting herself because, as she claims, he withdrew his affection for her and she could not live without him. In contrast, we interviewed a repeat offender in his forties who had a long and violent history of criminal activity. He shot and killed an elderly man while attempting to get him to open his safe. This particular offender is much different from the young man who shot and killed his stepfather after he had abused his mother and himself for many years. And that young man is as different from the methamphetamine user and seller we talked with who shot his girlfriend's sister when he was high and had not slept for two days. He had a long record of prior incarcerations for various other felonies. Despite the fact that we elicited responses to various important subjects from this sample of gun-using inmates, readers will have to make their own conclusions about the offenders whose accounts of their heinous crimes and perceptions of guns are reproduced in this book.

The voices of the gun offenders in this study provided us with insight into gun violence. We learned about their rationale for committing those crimes. Although the type of conflicting situations in which these offenders found themselves quite often made little sense to those of us looking in from the outside, we were able to gain some valuable insight into their beliefs and perceptions. Our findings describe the thought processes and various retrospective reinterpretations offered by these offenders for their particular use of a firearm in the commission of a crime. The findings paint a picture of how the offenders act and think in criminal situations.

Before we continue to describe the findings, we need to discuss the general methodological approach by which we carried out the research underlying this book. This will help orient readers to the context in which the details found in the inmates' accounts of guns and violence were obtained. More specifics regarding the methods as well as data collection and analytic procedures may be obtained in the Appendix at the end of this book.

Conducting any form of research in a prison—especially field-work—is problematic (Unnithan 1986). This is because the "correctional setting can affect the process of collecting data and the nature and quality of the information gathered" (Unnithan 1986:403). The first obstacle we had to overcome was the small group of correctional managers and state-level administrators who preside over Colorado's prison hierarchy. These high-level bureaucrats at the Colorado Department of Corrections are "gatekeepers" (see Broadhead and Rist 1976) to the prison system. They easily could have prevented us from gaining access to inmates and their prison files. Despite the fact that we had numerous connections to department personnel, and even though the federal government had funded this project through the US Attorney's Office for Colorado, gaining initial access to the prisons was noticeably difficult. The power to determine what prison research was valuable and permissible was the purview of the central office of the Colorado Department of Corrections and it was absolute. Although the executive director supported this project and gave us permission to conduct our research in the prisons, we experienced considerable difficulty in negotiating the bureaucracy of his office to arrange our access to inmates' prison files and to the far-flung research sites. Part of the problem was the complexity in determining who really made the ultimate decisions regarding access. In the end, we gained permission from a public corrections spokesperson to conduct the study after assurances from us that we were not "liberal pukes" as was imputed given our ivory-tower academic backgrounds.

Once we gained permission—and had an authority figure at the Colorado Department of Corrections as a "character reference"—we were able to comb through administrative records and contact each prison directly to set up the interviews. To our surprise, working with individual institutions across the state to arrange interviews with inmates could not have been easier. If the department saw us as a potential threat, this fear certainly was not shared among the local managers and staff of the various prisons we visited except in one case as noted below.

Research Setting

The research for this book was collected from interviews with inmates conducted in 11 different correctional facilities scattered throughout Colorado. Colorado's prison system is typical of most states and consists of 22 public (run by the state) and 7 private (administered by corporations under contract with the state) facilities that hold inmates convicted of various felonies. In 2007, there were approximately 22,424 inmates incarcerated in Colorado prisons. Similar to most states, Colorado has experienced prison population growth despite that fact that crime rates decreased through the late 1990s and early 2000s. For example, the number of inmates in Colorado prisons nearly doubled between 1997 and 2007. By the year 2011, Colorado estimates that its prison population will increase to approximately 30,000 inmates. In response, the state has increased its capacity to hold offenders through a prison construction boom. Since 1990, Colorado has built 12 new state-run prisons and contracted for 6 private prisons. The cost of this new prison construction is approximately $83,000 per bed. The state estimates that annual average operating costs will be $27,000 per bed (Colorado Department of Corrections 2004).

The large increase in Colorado's prison population is partially due to the increase in the number of female inmates. Between 1997 and 2007, the number of women incarcerated in Colorado prisons nearly tripled, from 3,370 to 9,567 inmates (Colorado Department of Corrections 2004). Most women are sent to prison for committing nonviolent crimes. For instance, approximately 76 percent of women incarcerated in Colorado are nonviolent, whereas violent offenses account for 24 percent of all females. This is especially true in the case of murder and robbery where firearms are more likely to be used. There were 23 female murder and robbery commitments in fiscal year 2005 and 20 commitments in fiscal year 2006 (Colorado Department of Corrections 2007). Men, on the other hand, had far more prison commitments for violent crimes than women, and nearly 200 were incarcerated for murder and robbery in fiscal years 2006 and 2007. This meant that the interviews were conducted mainly with male prisoners, though we did have several female prisoners in the sample.

To converse with and interview Colorado's inmates convicted of gun-related violent crimes and to learn about their place within the "gun culture," we traveled hundreds of miles back and forth across the state to visit them in the prisons where they were being held. Many of Colorado's prisons are located in relatively remote rural areas of the state such as Limon, in the vast Eastern Plains and close to the Kansas border; Cañon City, nestled high in the mountains; or Sterling, in the northeast corner of the square state. During the Colorado prison construction boom, rural counties competed for these projects, believing that prisons would bring jobs and economic development to their region (for a description of a similar approach in California, see Gilmore 2006). In our travels, we found some truth to these assertions. There were hotels and fast-food restaurants, many of them relatively new, located adjacent to various prisons. Several locals told us that business picked up during the weekends when families and friends from Denver or Colorado Springs came to meet with their incarcerated loved ones during prison visiting hours.

Due to the severe nature of the offenses we were studying, most of our time was spent talking with inmates located in Colorado's Security Level IV and Level V correction facilities, which are generally the most secure prisons in the state. These facilities became recognizable to us, as we drove toward them, because of the towers, walls, razor wire, and the continuous pickup truck patrols that monitored their perimeters. A few of the interviews, however, were conducted in low-security prisons. After spending a considerable amount of time interviewing in high-security prisons, doing the same in low-security prisons was a bit unnerving initially. Low-security prisons, often operated by private corporations, allowed us more freedom of movement. We commonly were instructed to find our way to various parts of a particular prison unescorted and, in some cases, unmonitored. In many instances, such trips led to interesting interactions and conversations with various prison staff members and inmates that we encountered. For example, private prison staff sometimes lamented their low pay and relative lack of benefits, contrasting them with the better salaries and benefits accorded to their peers at institutions run by the state.

We interviewed inmates at Colorado Department of Corrections facilities across the state that held inmates convicted of violent gun crimes (Security Levels II through V). The complexes that we visited for this project included Arkansas Valley, Bent, Buena Vista, Crowley County, East Complex, Limon, Sterling, Territorial, Trinidad, and Women's. Some of these complexes are the site of more than one prison facility. For example, the East Complex holds Arrowhead, Centennial, Colorado State Penitentiaries, Four Mile, and Fremont. In an effort to maintain confidentiality, if not absolute anonymity, we do not link the interviews with specific institutions.

For the most part, our introductory routines at each facility that we visited were similar and relatively uncomplicated. We notified the warden, appropriate prison staff, and inmates prior to our arrival at the prison to conduct the interviews. In most cases, the prison administration was able to accommodate our requests. In a few instances, however, the interview dates had to be changed to take into account prison-wide lockdowns or a warden who wanted to talk with us prior to the interviews, but was unavailable on the dates requested. Usually, the warden made arrangements to greet us as soon as we arrived at a prison. Our interactions with prison staff were generally pleasant and it was common for us to know at least one prison guard or staff member in each of the prisons that we visited. A few were former students who fortunately remembered their days on our respective campuses with affection. Indeed, we were often told by prison staff that they enjoyed having us visit their facility and wished that there were more such partnerships between researchers and prisons. In several instances, we were invited to dine in the prison cafeteria with the staff. Such meals provided us with time to talk with staff members about the prison and their experiences working in these institutions.

It is interesting to note that, although we originally thought that prison staff and administrators would be suspicious of our motivations for wanting to talk with their prisoners, we encountered outright hostility by only one such individual: a prison administrator who had complained loudly about academic researchers. In the first case, this administrator monitored us constantly during our visit. At one point, she interrupted an interview to take away a soda that the interviewer had purchased for the inmate. This put the interviewer in the awkward position of having to save face by sticking up for the inmate for fear of losing valuable information and jeopardizing future interviews in that institution. Although these types of experiences are uncomfortable, they are not unusual for deviance researchers. Accepting a stigma by association (or courtesy stigma) is often used to help establish rapport with subjects and improve the quality of the information we gather (Anderson and Calhoun 1992; Goffman 1963). In another instance, the same administrator disciplined a correctional officer directly in front of an interviewer for allowing an interview to be conducted with an inmate who was supposed to be in administrative segregation. Again, the interviewers were forced to intervene by claiming that they had misunderstood the rules about who could and could not be interviewed.

The interviews with inmates were conducted within the prison walls in private conference rooms, staff offices, or visitation rooms (when they were not being used). Before we entered these settings, we were required to undergo searches for any items that we may have been carrying that could be considered contraband under institutional rules. We were allowed to carry pens, pencils, paper, and tape recorders into the prison—all of which had to be accounted for before we left. In one instance, an interviewer tossed a few used tape recorder batteries in the trash can in a visitation room and was detained at the front gate for some time until the batteries could be searched for and recovered.

Sample of Violent Gun Offenders

We selected the inmates we interviewed for this study with the help of the Colorado Department of Corrections (see the Appendix at the back of the book). As we discovered, many of the interviewees had experienced previous encounters with law enforcement. For example, over two-thirds of all inmates we spoke with (77 percent) reported that they had been arrested for a felony at least once prior to their current criminal offense. Their prison files confirmed this information. In addition, nearly one-third (32.9 percent) had been incarcerated for a felony in the past. Most inmates had extensive experience with guns. Nearly 60 percent admitted to having used a gun in the past for legitimate or criminal purposes. Many who did not admit to past gun use had what they described as extended current involvement (i.e., several armed robberies). Finally, we discovered that nearly one-third (32.9 percent) of the sample had been affiliated with street gangs at some point in the past. Many of these gang members were incarcerated in the mid- to late 1990s when violent crime in Colorado was decreasing, but gang violence was viewed as a serious problem.

For the most part, the offenders we talked with used a variety of guns in the handgun category. Indeed, 94.6 percent of inmates reported that they had selected a handgun for their most recent offense. And nearly 50 percent of those inmates used .38- and .25-caliber handguns. Moreover, approximately one-half of the interviewees used what they described as semiautomatic weapons while the other half used revolvers. Despite claims that criminals are becoming "superarmed," we found little evidence that they had advanced weaponry of any sort (Johnson 2007).

We were surprised to learn that many of the inmates had held legitimate jobs that ranged from employment in the service sector (e.g., fast-food cook, cashier, and sales) to blue-collar work as mechanics, manufacturing workers, and welders to more white-collar jobs in administration. Some, though few, admitted to us that their main source of income was crime related (i.e., drug sales and robberies). We also were surprised to learn that nearly one-third of the subjects had children who they could claim as dependents. Moreover, in many instances, they kept in touch with the children on a regular basis.

The background characteristics of the Colorado gun offenders who we interviewed suggest that they are not that different from inmates incarcerated for gun offenses in other states. Thus, these inmates' beliefs, attitudes, and perceptions are likely to be similar to inmates in other states.

We began each interview with a brief explanation about how inmates were selected for the study and the types of topics that we might discuss. We told inmates that their participation in this research project was entirely voluntary and that they were under no obligation to answer any of our inquiries. We informed them that, if they felt uncomfortable with any of the topics of discussion, they could simply tell us that and we would proceed to other topics and related inquiries. Moreover, we clearly stated that inmates could end the interview whenever they wished. Throughout the interview process, we made every effort to ensure that inmates understood that our conversations were both voluntary and confidential. We told each inmate that no one except us would be able to identify their answers and that any information they provided to us would be used only for research purposes. Finally, we emphasized that we did not want any details, if any, that might compromise an inmate's pending legal case. It is important to point out that we did discover—through our conversations with interviewees—that inmates who met our criteria but refused to be interviewed were mainly concerned with potential legal repercussions. And in one case, an interviewer was told that an inmate who recently had been incarcerated for the first time was just "too scared" to talk with him. Still, we have good reason to believe that most of the inmates we interviewed were surprisingly open and honest about their past behavior. Again, we are confident in the validity of the data because inmates often gave answers that closely matched information that was available and recorded in their prison file. Lastly, we should point out that a few inmates who felt uncomfortable with a particular line of questioning asked the interviewer to momentarily turn off the tape recorder so that their responses would not be recorded. These brief unrecorded conversations often were focused on a particular aspect of that inmate's crime and were largely inconsequential to the current research questions. A small number of inmates did not allow us to tape any part of their interviews. However, the majority of inmates seemed eager to talk to us despite the presence of the tape recorder.

Inmate interviews lasted between 60 and 120 minutes, though some interviews ran a little longer. Because this study was cross-sectional in nature, inmates were interviewed at different points in their sentences. Thus, similar to many criminological studies, we often drew on cross-sectional data to simulate longitudinal results (Hirschi and Gottfredson 1990). Data were gathered primarily through semi-structured interviews with inmates. Interviews were organized around a list of topics that covered a variety of issues surrounding gun use and violence. Responses to interviewers' inquiries were open ended and inmates could freely relate their responses. The issues we discussed during the conversations with inmates relied heavily on our own interpersonal interview styles (Fontana and Frey 1994; Minichiello et al. 1995). Thus, although we had topics to cover, no questions or probes were strictly predetermined, sequenced, or standardized. Instead, we allowed the inmate to control the flow of conversation on each topic while casually inquiring about guns as and where appropriate. There are many benefits of this type of information gathering. Specifically, the greater degree of informality involved led to a stronger rapport between the inmate and interviewer. Further, inmates were allowed to express themselves in ways that are natural to them (Burns 2000) as opposed to being led, prepared, or directed by the interviewer.

We asked the interviewees general issues about their family, schools, peer group, neighborhood, prior contact with the criminal justice system, and experiences with firearms. Inmates were also asked about a series of events surrounding the circumstances that led up to the crime for which they were currently incarcerated. It was from this vantage point that we began to see the importance of gangs and prison socialization in influencing the interviewees' perceptions about guns. When details we were interested in were left out of the conversation, we often used the information gleaned from the interviewee's prison file as a probe to initiate dialogue on those subjects. In most cases, the interviewee's knowledge that we had information from the file in our possession appeared to move the discussions forward rather than shutting them down.

We chose to introduce each inmate in the sample to readers in Table 1.1 so that they can get a sense of the inmate's background as they read the book. Table 1.1 displays general information about the inmates, including their pseudonym (to ensure that they cannot be identified), crime, gang status, and general demographics. The table also notes various differences such as gang membership. As the table demonstrates, the median age of the 24 gang members in the sample is 25, though their age at the time they committed their violent crime was considerably younger. Thirteen of those gang members are black, five are white, two are Asian, and four are Hispanic. Seven of the gang members we interviewed were convicted of murder or non-negligent manslaughter, six were convicted of attempted murder, two were convicted of robbery, seven were convicted of assault, and two were convicted of kidnapping. At the time of the interviews, the inmates had been incarcerated for an average of 4.7 years. All but two

Table 1.1　List of Interviewed Inmates by Crime, Gun Use, Gang Membership, and Demographics (*n* = 73; mean age = 32.93)

Tape	Pseudonym	Current Crime	Gun Used in Current Crime	Age When Interviewed	Sex	Race	Street Gang Member	Arrested in Prior Offense	Previous Prison Sentence	Previous Gun Experience/ Use (Self-Admit)
1	Isaiah	Robbery	Handgun	25	Male	White	No	No	No	No
2	Ernesto	Robbery	Handgun	28	Male	Hispanic	No	Yes	No	No
3	Edwin	Homicide	Handgun	53	Male	White	No	No	No	Yes
4	Claude	Other	Handgun	32	Male	Black	Yes	Yes	No	No
5	Charles	Assault	Handgun	55	Male	Black	No	Yes	Yes	Yes
6	Elton	Robbery	Handgun	32	Male	Black	No	Yes	No	Yes
7	Jan	Homicide	Handgun	26	Male	Hispanic	No	Yes	No	Yes
8	Willian	Other	Handgun	38	Male	White	No	Yes	No	Yes
9	Reinaldo	Kidnapping	Handgun	23	Male	Hispanic	No	Yes	Yes	Yes
10	Bob	Robbery	Handgun	43	Male	Hispanic	No	Yes	Yes	Yes
11	Damon	Other	Handgun	43	Male	Hispanic	No	No	No	No
12	David	Other	Handgun	33	Male	Black	Yes	Yes	No	Yes
13	Johnathan	Assault	Shotgun	36	Male	White	No	Yes	Yes	Yes
14	Russ	Homicide	Handgun	43	Male	Black	No	Yes	No	Yes

15	Len	Homicide	Handgun	30	Male	Black	No	Yes	No	Yes
16	Zack	Robbery	Handgun	35	Male	Black	No	Yes	No	Yes
17	Tim	Assault	Handgun	38	Male	White	Yes	Yes	Yes	Yes
18	Antwan	Other	Handgun	32	Male	White	No	No	Yes	Yes
19	Chance	Robbery	Handgun	35	Male	Black	No	Yes	No	No
20	Jerry	Homicide	Handgun	27	Male	Black	No	No	No	Yes
21	Stephen	Homicide	Handgun	51	Male	Other	No	No	No	No
22	Mike	Homicide	Handgun	25	Male	Black	Yes	Yes	Yes	Yes
23	Miquel	Assault	Handgun	23	Male	Black	Yes	Yes	No	No
24	Marc	Homicide	Handgun	55	Male	White	No	No	No	No
25	Darrel	Homicide	Handgun	28	Male	White	No	Yes	No	No
26	Orval	Other	Handgun	28	Male	Hispanic	Yes	Yes	Yes	Yes
27	Charlie	Kidnapping	Handgun	21	Male	Black	Yes	Yes	Yes	Yes
28	Logan	Homicide	Handgun	28	Male	White	Yes	Yes	Yes	Yes
29	Hollis	Homicide	Handgun	67	Male	White	No	Yes	Yes	No
30	Windord	Assault	Handgun	43	Male	White	Yes	Yes	Yes	Yes
31	Trent	Homicide	Handgun	33	Male	Black	No	Yes	Yes	Yes
32	Langley	Assault	Handgun	21	Male	White	No	Yes	No	Yes
33	Sidney	Homicide	Handgun	32	Male	Black	Yes	No	No	Yes
34	Casey	Robbery	Handgun	28	Male	White	No	No	No	No
35	Ricardo	Homicide	Handgun	21	Male	Black	Yes	Yes	No	No
36	Jack	Other	Handgun	35	Male	Hispanic	No	Yes	Yes	Yes
37	Giselle	Other	Handgun	26	Female	Hispanic	Yes	Yes	No	Yes

continues

Table 1.1 continued

Tape	Pseudonym	Current Crime	Gun Used in Current Crime	Age When Interviewed	Sex	Race	Street Gang Member	Arrested in Prior Offense	Previous Prison Sentence	Previous Gun Experience/ Use (Self-Admit)
38	Tiffiny	Homicide	Handgun	24	Female	White	No	No	No	No
39	Vicky	Robbery	Handgun	20	Female	Black	No	Yes	No	No
40	Maryland	Robbery	Handgun	26	Female	Black	Yes	No	No	Yes
41	Sandy	Homicide	Handgun	33	Female	Black	No	No	No	No
42	Donald	Homicide	Handgun	33	Male	Black	No	No	No	Yes
43	Baxter	Robbery	Handgun	50	Male	White	No	Yes	Yes	No
44	Newton	Homicide	Handgun	38	Male	Black	Yes	Yes	Yes	Yes
45	Renato	Homicide	Handgun	60	Male	White	No	Yes	Yes	Yes
46	Elbert	Other	Handgun	43	Male	Hispanic	No	Yes	No	No
47	Rodney	Robbery	Handgun	21	Male	White	No	Yes	No	Yes
48	Francesco	Homicide	Handgun	27	Male	White	No	No	No	No
49	Mark	Other	Handgun	20	Male	Black	Yes	Yes	No	Yes
50	Cleveland	Robbery	Handgun	21	Male	White	No	Yes	No	No
51	Gerry	Assault	Handgun	23	Male	White	Yes	Yes	No	No
52	Pete	Assault	Handgun	29	Male	Hispanic	Yes	Yes	Yes	Yes

#	Name	Crime	Weapon	Age	Sex	Race			
53	Clifford	Robbery	Handgun	50	Male	White	No	Yes	No	Yes
54	Ken	Other	Handgun	25	Male	White	No	Yes	No	Yes
55	Kent	Homicide	Rifle	28	Male	Hispanic	No	Yes	Yes	No
56	Paul	Homicide	Handgun	21	Male	Black	No	Yes	No	No
57	Wiley	Assault	Handgun	22	Male	Black	Yes	Yes	No	Yes
58	Arturo	Kidnapping	Handgun	20	Male	Other	Yes	No	No	No
59	Thad	Robbery	Handgun	33	Male	Black	No	No	Yes	Yes
60	Beau	Robbery	Handgun	24	Male	White	Yes	Yes	No	Yes
61	Trey	Homicide	Handgun	23	Male	Black	Yes	Yes	No	No
62	Preston	Assault	Shotgun	23	Male	White	No	Yes	No	No
63	Matthew	Homicide	Handgun	42	Male	Black	No	Yes	No	Yes
64	Lance	Robbery	Handgun	56	Male	White	No	Yes	Yes	Yes
65	Dan	Homicide	Handgun	21	Male	Other	Yes	Yes	No	No
66	Wade	Homicide	Handgun	27	Male	Black	No	Yes	No	No
67	Frederic	Assault	Handgun	25	Male	Black	Yes	Yes	Yes	Yes
68	Carlo	Homicide	Rifle	38	Male	White	No	Yes	No	No
69	Doug	Other	Handgun	32	Male	White	No	Yes	Yes	Yes
70	Reed	Homicide	Handgun	64	Male	White	No	No	No	No
71	Eloy	Other	Handgun	21	Male	Hispanic	Yes	Yes	No	Yes
72	Sam	Homicide	Handgun	50	Male	Black	No	Yes	No	No
73	Brandee	Robbery	Handgun	19	Female	White	No	No	No	No

in the sample of gang members are male, and all of the gang members used a handgun in the commission of the crime for which they are currently incarcerated.

Approach

Qualitative research has clearly witnessed a resurgence in popularity over the past decade in all of the various social sciences (Bryman and Burgess 1994; Hess-Biber and Leavy 2008). More recently, there has been an increase in the literature that encourages and promotes qualitative research techniques to gain a more comprehensive understanding of social problems, such as gun use, and their various manifestations. Denzin and Lincoln offer their perspective as to why qualitative methods have become more pervasive of late.

> In more than two decades a quiet methodological revolution has been taking place in the social sciences. A blurring of disciplinary boundaries has occurred. The social sciences and humanities have drawn closer together in mutual focus on an interpretive, qualitative approach to research and theory. Although these trends are not new, the extent to which the qualitative revolution has overtaken the social sciences and related professional fields has been nothing short of amazing. (1998:vii)

The reason for the qualitative approach in this work is, of course, to present in-depth knowledge necessary to portray the inmates' perspectives about guns through their social locations as they experience them (Glaser and Strauss 1967; Pogrebin 2003). Thus, the strength of this work stems from its inductive approach and emphasis on specific situations, and the utilization of language rather than numerical explanations (Maxwell 1996). This research stresses interpretive, ethnographic methods that provide for insightful and contextual knowledge at close range (Daly and Chesney-Lind 1988). Therefore, we focus on the narrative accounts of inmates to explain their gun use. The use of narrative accounts is a strategic method by which we ask the interviewees to relate their violent past. Narrative analysis is often described as a successful approach that can be used to study controversial and difficult topics (Migliaccio 2002). A narrative format can provide rich and detailed data, which may lead to insights into the connections between one's life experiences and social environment (Pierce 2003). Narrative analysis, notes Pierce, explains how people strategize and act within the context of their past interpersonal experiences. Relating stories through narratives is a type of social interaction where the primary purpose is to construct and communicate meaning. Chase argues that such a forum "draws on and is constrained by the culture by which it is embedded" (1995:7). Walzer and Oles (2003) point out that explanations may reflect attempts to maintain face to convince the audience that we are okay by framing our actions in terms of what we perceive to be acceptable. The advantage of this approach in our research is that, once we had established rapport with the interviewees, the lengthy interviews gave them the opportunity and conversational latitude needed to discuss their ideas and perceptions about guns.

The interview tapes were transcribed for qualitative data analysis, which involves scanning and identifying general statements about relationships among categories of observations. We looked for explanations concerning inmates' perceptions about the importance of guns as Schatzman and Strauss (1973) suggest.

Hobbs and May (1993) contend that in-depth interviews are the best way to gather data that could never be obtained by only observing the activities of people. Given the fact that intensive interviews are often part of participant observation, we argue that they are sufficient to make conclusions regarding accounts of behavior, perceptions of guns and gun laws, and gang socialization. It is to these tasks that we now turn.

Organization of the Book

In Chapter 2, we examine why the inmates we interviewed say they used guns in the commission of their offenses. Through our conversations with the inmates, we discovered that offenders are able to utilize a repertoire of accounts to explain their gun violence. As readers will note, the inmates frequently utilize both fact and fantasy when explaining why they used guns. We discovered that most inmates explain their gun use through what Scott and Lyman (1968) famously term "justifications" and "excuses." Our experiences with gun-using inmates suggest that these accounts were effective in preserving their conventional sense of self, self-concept, or identity. In fact, it often was not until we read through the transcripts of the interviews that we realized how untoward and socially unacceptable many acts narrated by a given inmate actually were.

This is not to say that we were "fooled" by inmates' descriptions of events since we had prior access to their prison files and all of the life history and criminal event information contained therein. More specifically, we placed each interviewee's summary "rap sheet" on the table where we conducted our conversations in a way that was visible to the interviewee. Even though the files provided us with an adequate picture of each inmate before the interviews and, given the physical presence of the rap sheet, the inmate was aware that we knew about his or her previous history, there nevertheless was some vagueness and ambiguity in each file that allowed the inmate some conversational space to locate his or her conventional self. Our jobs, as interviewers, were to allow these types of interactions and to permit the inmates to put their best face forward during the interviews. Thus, we were engaged in their explanations of events and were outwardly accepting of their excuses and justifications. In parallel with such seeming acceptance, we probed them actively, extensively, and, when indicated, rather skeptically for more details about guns in the crimes they had committed and in their everyday lives.

In Chapter 3, we investigate the potential role of guns in producing and reproducing violent norms in street gang cultures. Many of the inmates we interviewed came from social and cultural locations that increased the probability of their joining and participating in a street gang. Although some inmates were in a gang and some were not, we did notice that gang members' experiences and perceptions of guns were quite different from the inmates who were raised in non-gang neighborhoods and settings. Moreover, inmates enmeshed in the street gang culture told us that the gun was a potent symbol of power and a ready remedy for all manner of conflicts and disputes.

These explanations remind us of a large amount of recent work in criminology suggesting that an individual's reputation is extremely important and that violence is one major way to project a tough reputation. We believe that guns serve as symbols and tools that may help project, establish, and maintain such a reputation. Thus, we focus on the issue of gang socialization and the central role that guns play in that process. We believe that American society may have underestimated the extent to which guns influence gang socialization and therefore also the symbolic impact of guns on violent behavior and individual identities in such contexts.

In Chapter 4, we explore inmate perceptions about the reasons that other people in society carry guns. Although most other people say that they carry guns for self-protection, power, or both, during the interviews we began to notice that inmates' accounts varied according to the number of years they had been imprisoned. This finding, grounded in the conversations with inmates, is interesting to us because it suggests that incarceration can change an inmate's views about guns. Even as the issues of prison socialization and its consequences have been debated for some time in the sociological literature, we believe that prisons may increase rather than decrease the probability that former inmates will use guns after their release from incarceration. Just as the interviewees were socialized on the street, they also have been socialized during their time in the prison. This latter socialization process is important if we wish to understand why inmates may leave prison only to revert to using guns again in the future.

In Chapter 5, we examine the interviewees' attitudes regarding gun laws. Many inmates brought up the issue of Colorado's gun laws during their interviews and wanted us to know how they felt about those laws. In Colorado, gun legislation and associated policies are designed by politicians in the state legislature who pay close attention to their constituents' views about firearms. One recently popular form of gun policy in a majority of states consists of the so-called shall-issue laws for carrying concealed weapons. Colorado had debated just such a law in Senate Bill 03-024 of 2003 (since enacted into law as Section 18-12-2 of the Colorado Revised Statutes).

Moreover, though issues pertaining to the freedom and regulation surrounding the possession and use of firearms have always been controversial in the United States (Utter 2000; Wilson 2006), few researchers have asked inmates who have used guns in the commission of a violent crime about their views of shall-issue policies. Of course, though we cannot claim that the inmates we talked with were truthful about what they said they would do "on the street" in response to shall-issue gun laws, we did find that inmates hold both positive and negative views of Colorado's gun policy. Rather alarmingly, the majority of inmates told us they would act more aggressively if they knew that others with whom they interacted were likely to be carrying concealed weapons. A minority of inmates said they would act less aggressively in similar situations.

This chapter has provided an overview of the topics and issues that we will discuss in the four substantive chapters that follow.

Chapter 6, our final chapter, brings together the major conclusions of the various substantive chapters. In it, we also seek to answer several additional questions regarding the place of guns in the commission of criminal violence and, more generally, in relation to criminal behavior. Conclusions from our overall research project and their theoretical and methodological implications are presented along with suggestions for future research.

2

Motives for
Criminal Gun Use

THE GUN OFFENDERS IN THIS STUDY PROVIDED SEVERAL MOTIVES for their violent crimes. In this chapter, we focus on the reasons that offenders say they used a gun in violent acts. We employ the notion of "accounts" to relate offender narratives. Scott and Lyman first introduced their concept of accounts in 1968. They explain that an *account* is simply a "linguistic device" that an individual uses to explain deviant behavior (1968:219). When used convincingly, accounts can effectively blur the distinction between "appearances and reality, truth and falsity, triviality and importance, accident and essence, coincidence and cause" (Garfinkel 1956:420). It should come as no surprise that sociologists have used the concept of accounts to examine a variety of behaviors such as HIV risk taking (Fontdevila, Bassel, and Gilbert 2005), Medicare or Medicaid fraud (Evans and Porche 2005), computer hacking (Turgeman-Goldschmidt 2005), intimate partner violence (Wood 2004), violent crime (Presser 2004), rape (Scully and Marolla 1984), child abandonment (Geiger and Fischer 2003), snitching (Pershing 2003), steroid use (Monaghan 2002), and white-collar crime (Willott, Griffin, and Torrance 2001). This is not surprising because the stories people use are often similar and tell us something interesting and unique about our culture. Thus, the study of accounts allows for understanding and unique "insight into the human experience [in order to] arrive at . . . culturally embedded normative explanations" (Orbuch 1997:455). We were intrigued by the interviewees' accounts of gun violence and, therefore, focus on those accounts in this chapter.

As noted in Chapter 1, narrative analysis is often described as a successful approach that can be used to study controversial and difficult topics (Migliaccio 2002). Thus, we often began our interviews by asking the inmates how they ended up in prison. It was clear to us from the outset that the interviewees believed we would form moral judgments about their character based on their response to the question: How did you get here? They answered by giving us descriptions that they believed would resonate. Thus, most inmates engaged in what Gross and Stone (1964) call a "performance norm," where we (as researchers) allowed them an opportunity to adopt a conventional role and explain their gun violence. Indeed, most conversations were quite natural and proceeded as if we were chatting with a new acquaintance at a coffee shop or other meeting place. It is within this context that the interviewees provided us with accounts of their gun violence.

Accounts Versus the Etiology of Crime

Prior to presenting the inmate accounts, we must clarify some important aspects of accounts. We begin with the observations of Mills who notes that "the differing reasons men give for their actions are not themselves without reasons" (1940:904). Mills makes a sharp distinction between "cause" and "explanation" and, therefore, focuses on the reasons individuals give for their actions. Thus, we do not seek answers to the etiology of gun violence in this chapter. Rather, we are concerned with the way inmates express themselves while accounting for their violent behavior. How will an inmate's motive appear to others? Mills argues that people often express themselves in "special vocabularies" that must account for past, present, or future behavior (1940:904). Thus, inmates in our study were likely attempting to shape our view of their intent or motivation for using a gun by explaining how their situation was unique and could be justified or excused. The hope, of course, was that this would prevent their personal devaluation, a stigma, or the imposition of negative sanctions.

It is no doubt true that, in many instances, being able to effectively present accounts of deviant behavior will lessen the degree of one's moral responsibility. Indeed, most inmates were able to draw from a repertoire of accounts in explaining their gun violence. As researchers, we did not challenge those reasons as insincere or deny the validity of their claims; they may well have committed their violent act for the very reasons that they provided.

Accounts are, above all, a form of *impression management* that represents a mixture of fact and fantasy. Goffman (1959), for example, argues that social behavior involves a great deal of deliberate deception as self-impressions are continually created, managed, and presented to others. Briefly, we "put on a face to meet the faces we meet." Because others often judge accounts for authenticity, determining if the mixture of fact and fantasy will be accepted as a legitimate excuse or justification can be difficult. We believe that the inmates we interviewed felt it was important that we interpret their accounts as an honest and sufficient indicator of their intentions, motivations, beliefs, and values (i.e., their character). Consequently, we argue, like Goffman, that the interviewees had to appear genuine in their self-presentations and we had to appear willing to accept their reasons. As Gross and Stone (1964) point out, each participant in an interaction must present a construction of self that complements the others who are engaged in that interaction. These interactions helped the interviewees portray prosocial behavior when accounting for their gun violence. Although inmates are frequently described as uncaring sociopaths, we found, like Tedeschi and Riordan (1981), that most interviewees tried with great care to affirm their commitment to conventional values and goals in order to win our acceptance. Similar to the finding of Prus (1975), the interviewees often sought our feedback to determine whether we were accepting their excuses and justifications. And being professional interviewers, we obliged. As Jones and Pittman note, "to the extent that the threatened sustains his counteractive behavior or to the extent that the counteractive behavior involves effort and costly commitments, social confirmation will have the restorative power sought" (1982:255–256).

In almost every account, we found that inmates tried to maintain a normal presentation of self within an abnormal situation. They desperately wanted us to see their past criminal behavior as atypical (i.e., that it is not indicative of his or her true self). For example, Wade, a 27-year-old convicted of murder, tells about the event.

WADE: He reached down like that I figure, he had a gun himself because he's an ex-military. He's got a license to carry a gun. And then at that time, a person there that night had a pistol with him. I just grabbed it and I just shot him. I tried to avoid it, but it just happened. It happened so fast. I'm not a bad person. I didn't have no criminal records at all and I was just at the wrong place at the wrong time.

INTERVIEWER: So this was your first offense?

WADE: Yes.

INTERVIEWER: So was this a struggle?

WADE: No.

INTERVIEWER: Were there other situations before?

WADE: I never had problems. That was the first person I ever had problems with. As growing up, I don't go out there looking for problems.

In some cases, inmates would even freely admit the error of their ways and accept the moral responsibility of their violence, but without accepting a deviant identity (because the situation clearly demanded such action). However, many inmates did not appear to us to be concerned with questions of morality about their actions. Instead, they were extremely concerned about presenting a moral self. Inmates presented accounts of gun violence in one of two ways: through justifications or through excuses. In the remainder of this chapter, we examine the accounts in terms of justifications and excuses (for a legal distinction between these two concepts, see Brody, Acker, and Logan 2001). We use the classic work of Scott and Lyman (1968) to guide a sociological discussion of accounts as either justifications or excuses. Scott and Lyman identify the kind of talk that is meant to explain the void between actions and societal expectations as an account for deviant behavior by a person who attempts to offer explanations for their criminal acts. Justifications and excuses are efforts to reconstruct social perceptions of wrongful behavior. We need to point out that, in many cases, the inmates' justifications were successful in the sense that we as interviewers were drawn into the situation leading up to their crime—we wanted desperately to believe that their actions did not represent who they really are.

Justifications

Justifications are "accounts in which one accepts responsibility for the act in question, but denies the pejorative quality associated with it" (Scott and Lyman 1968:47). There are five ideal types of justifications presented by Scott and Lyman that we found inmates drew on in their stories about how they arrived in prison. These justifications include denial of victim, denial of injury, appeal to higher loyalties, condemnation of condemners, and sad tales. Each justification is explained in more detail below. It is important to point out that, although justifications are often described as ideal types in the literature, they often are more complex in real life. Inmates were likely to use several justifications (and excuses—see below) when telling us how they arrived in prison.

Denial of Victim

The most common justification for violent gun use among our sample of inmates is denial of victim. Scott and Lyman (1968) found that individuals who employ this justification argue that the victim deserved the injury. They often try to make a case that their shooting was in "self-defense." Thus, many of the inmates in our study maintain that their gun use was justified because the victim deserved to be shot. We present five inmate narratives below to illustrate the diverse ways that interviewees claim that the victim was responsible for their injury. We focus most of the narrative on this particular justification because it is used so pervasively in our sample. In the first case, Damon shot his supervisor for terminating his employment. He recalls the humiliation he felt because of his supervisor's actions. In the second case, Orval explains that the victim physically threatened him and stole his drugs. Thus, to Orval, the victim was not a victim, but a potentially violent criminal who deserved to be shot. In the third case, Zack shot his victim for failing to "play by the rules" and acknowledge the power that Zack had as a result of possessing a gun. The victim in Zack's case clearly could have prevented his injury simply by acting in a rational fashion. In the fourth case, Francesco argues that the victim was dangerous because he was not thinking straight and was going to harm him. Each story is different but, in all cases, the account is justified by the victim's actions or conditions.

Our first narrative examines Damon's justification for shooting his boss through use of a denial of victim justification. In his account, Damon claims that his boss was lazy, a bully, and mean.

DAMON: I got tired. I had been working a long time for that company. Then, one day one of the tenants had not paid their rent so they decided to put their belongings on the street. So we went with the sheriff and started carrying chairs, tables, that kind of stuff. There were other people that were supposed to be helping me. That would be my supervisor and another maintenance guy. I told my supervisor—his name is Robert—"Aren't you supposed to be helping me, man?" He put his face in front of mine and said, "You know what, you work for me!" He said, "You do not have to tell me what I have to do. Okay?" So, I got very upset because nobody yells in my face like this before. So I point my finger close to his face and started laughing, you know. He said, "That's okay I will see you crying in five minutes." After that, I went to clean the swimming pool. I got a call on my radio that told me to come to the office. Robert said, "Give me your keys, your radio, and the beeper." So when this happens he said, "Good luck"—meaning that I was fired. He fired me on the spot. I was very upset. The money I was making at the apartment complex was to help my family in Colombia. The guy had to pay for what he did. I wanted to explode you know. I had a .38-caliber gun in my car. When I grabbed the weapon, I knew I was ready. When I approached him [Robert], I had a sport magazine and I covered the weapon with it. I was approaching him, but the other maintenance man became suspicious. He said, "Robert, watch out!" When he said that, "Boom"—I shot him. I sat down and waited for the police. It was a relief for me. You feel rested.

Damon had no prior criminal history. The demeaning incident that led up to the shooting of his supervisor was associated with the humiliation that he experienced from his supervisor's confrontational interaction. Damon notes two important occurrences that took place prior to the shooting. First, his supervisor spoke harshly to him up close to his face, thus violating his personal space that should be respected by another during face-to-face interaction. Second, his supervisor abruptly fired him from a job he had held for seven years. It was clear to us that Damon harbors a deep sense of anger over the two confrontations with his supervisor. He clearly discusses his anger and desire for retaliation when he makes the point that he was so angry that he felt like he was going to explode. He explains that his supervisor would have to pay for his actions. It is at this point in the account that Damon justifies committing attempted murder. He also accounts for his actions by arguing that the loss of his job would adversely impact his family who still resided in Colombia. In short, from this offender's perspective, the victim was responsible for his injury.

After the shooting incident was over, Damon says that he sat down and waited for the police. He expresses a sense of relief and claims that he felt rested. The actual retaliatory incident rapidly decreased his rage. He did what he had to do to vindicate the anger he experienced because of the victim. However, nowhere in our interview did Damon claim that his violent actions were righteous. Instead, he laid claims and attempted to portray himself as a person who, at the time, needed to redeem his sense of self by causing pain and physical harm to the person who had committed a terrible wrong against him.

Orval, a gang member, was robbed of a considerable amount of drugs he was going to sell. He describes his conflict about whether he should shoot the robber or not. But he also accounts for his decision to kill to get back his drugs or the money they were worth. By sharing his conflict with the interviewer, he reiterates his dilemma. Orval also claims that, although the victim stole from him, the action that cost the victim his life was the threat of harm.

ORVAL: I had a gun in my pocket and I told him, you know, "Why did you jack us?" And he [victim] tried to play it off like he didn't know what I was talking about. I says, "You owe me $18,000 or you're gonna give me back my dope." And he says, "Hey, you come over here running your mouth again, I'll put a fucking hole in your head." So when he threatened me like that, I turned around, pulled out my gun, and walked right up to him and shot him in the head. When he hit the ground, I shot him two or three more times. . . . I was selling drugs. Drugs was my life. And when he went in there and jacked us for dope, he was taking away from how I made my living. Word gets back on the street that me and my partner had got jacked, everybody's waiting to see what we're going to do. If we didn't do nothing, everybody else, everybody would come and rob us. It was like "Damn, what am I gonna do?" Some of it did have to do with peer pressure, but they didn't make me do it. But the man threatened my life and, you know, that's not good to threaten people's lives.

In a nutshell, Orval could either lose face as a gang member and drug dealer or do something to gain respect in the drug/gang community. Orval argues that his only option was to retaliate against the robber because the robber had both threatened his livelihood and showed him a considerable amount of disrespect by threatening to harm him in front of other people. Yet he accounts for shooting the robber to us by arguing that "people should not threaten other people's lives." Orval is clearly expressing that he had little choice within a limited set of possible actions. He could lose face and have nothing left of his gang member identity or cause harm to the person who had wronged him (Jacobs, Topalli, and Wright 2003). Here, he presents a self that needed to maintain a street gang image. From Orval's point of view, there appeared to be no alternative course of action than to shoot the victim.

As we discuss in greater detail in Chapter 3, the imprisoned gang members in this study who had been involved in violent gun encounters all expressed the importance of not losing face among their peers. The code of retaliation for both gang members and nongang members was sincerely believed to represent an ongoing presentation of self as tough and fearless. This image often leads to violent gun use over the most incidental actions that are interpreted as disrespectful. Being disrespectful was often viewed as an act that deserved retaliation. This same presentation of self continued and was often exacerbated by gangs of all races and ethnicities within the prisons that we visited.

In case after case, we heard the interviewees voice that, "If you carry a gun, you must be willing to use it." These justifications were often related to the denial of victim in which the inmate admitted to committing the violent act, but also argued that the victim caused him or her to use a gun. In other words, the injury would not have occurred except for the victim's actions. In the following account Zack, who was 28 years old at the time of the shooting, uses the denial of victim justification to explain his actions.

ZACK: I guess there are loner criminals out there but, for me, there are two or three guys. I really didn't do a lot of crime by myself. We would need some money for whatever reason and then, you know, "Hey man, where can we get some money?" We go rob it. We done convenience stores, liquor stores, any places we really thought had some decent money. . . . Well, I get out of the military and me, my brother, a friend of mine, and a friend of his decided to do a robbery. We had an interaction with some other young people and we both stopped at a light. We got into an interaction, and I pulled out my gun and shot the guy in the stomach. I was gonna fight him, but I had a gun. Why fight, you know, when you have a gun? My brother looks at me and says, "Man, you're a real killer now, aren't you?" I says, "No, I'm not, but if you got a weapon you might as well use it to protect yourself." I still had a sense of trying to do the right thing. I shot a warning shot up in the air to get him [victim] away from the car. He stood there. He started talking trash, and I just jammed the gun into his belly and pulled the trigger. He fell to the ground. We drove off, and went and pulled a robbery. I was arrested and I am doing time for attempted murder.

Zack claims that he tried to do the "right thing" by firing a warning shot to let the victim know he was serious in his demand to back down. In similar cases throughout the study, we found instances where victims threatened with a gun were shot when they failed to comply with the warnings given by the shooter. As in Zack's case, this usually occurred when the perpetrator actually feared physical retaliation from the victim. Zack clearly asks, Why fight someone when you possess a gun? Or, put another way, Why take the chance of being physically overpowered and humiliated in front of your peers when you can avoid a threatening situation by harming the aggressing victim before he harms you?

While relating his account of the events that led up to and followed the violent encounter, Zack offers two factors that tend to bolster his self-image as a bad ass (Katz 1988). First, his younger brother's admiration of him as a "real killer" seems to have masked his feelings of cowardice from shooting the unarmed victim instead of physically fighting him. And second, Zack presents a self that is in control of his emotions because he goes on after the shooting to commit an armed robbery. In short, he did not allow the emotional response associated with a possible homicide to interfere with his original mission to rob a business for money.

Francesco, who was 16 at the time he committed his murder, was incarcerated as a result of a confrontation with three African American teens. As Francesco explains, he likely would have retreated from a potential confrontation had he not been in possession of a loaded gun that he could brandish from relative safety toward his aggressors.

FRANCESCO: I kept the gun in the house most of the time. But this night that this happened, I had it in my car with me under the seat. On my way to work, I'm driving through the middle of a black neighbor-hood and there's these three guys out on the street corner jumping out in the middle of the street throwing rocks at cars. So this guy jumps out in the street at me throwing a rock over the hood of my car. So, right away, I make a U-turn right in the middle of the street. And I'm going back to confront him like, "What are you doing? Why are you guys out here yelling and all that?" His partner threw something else over the top of the car. I didn't see what it was—like a rock or some-thing. So I make another U-turn to where they were on the right side. I stopped the car and we got . . . got into this big argument and it escalates from there. I start to ask them why they are throwing rocks and stuff like that—jumping out into the middle of the street at cars—and they are acting all crazy and cussing at me. So they start to approach the car and I pull out my gun. In my mind, I'm figuring I'm going to scare them away. I never figured on shooting anybody. When I pulled out the gun, one of them kinda backed up behind the bushes, but the other two were still standing kinda tough. The guy I ended up shooting, he was still talking to me this whole time, still cussing at me and calling me racial names and that type of stuff. I had the gun out telling him to stop, you know, "I'll shoot you, if you don't stop coming toward the car." He's like, "Well, if you're gonna do it, just do it. If not, just drive away." I'm sitting there all confused now because I'm like, "This guy thinks he's superman or something." I couldn't figure out why he wasn't scared of the gun. I looked back at him. He jumped towards the car like I don't know if he was going to come through the window, or open the door and go for the gun. But as I look, he jumps toward me and I jerked the trigger one time and it ended up hitting him in the middle of the chest. I can see him grab himself and kind of start to go down. I drove off right away.

Francesco claims that the firearm caused him to have a false sense of bravado. And he implies that, if he had not taken his gun with him, he would not have confronted the victim. The gun, as was true in many other cases in this study, allows the instigator to have a self-percep-tion as a powerful person: one who can pull the weapon out during a conflict and make a more physical, threatening individual back down. This sense of power over another was exemplified in Francesco's case. The gun gives an advantage to the more vulnerable party (Francesco), and more than evens the odds that there will be no phys-ical threat to him. Yet the threat of a weapon does not always provide the desired end result. This and other cases that we analyzed sometimes saw the victim pursue the gun carrier despite the threat of severe physical harm or death. Once the victim does not adhere to the gun carrier's threats, the self-perception of power on the part of the instigator immediately changes. Francesco expresses this feeling when he says that he could not understand why the threat of pointing the gun did not prevent the victim from leaving the scene afraid. At this moment, Francesco's account is formulated. He argues that, if only the victim had reacted with fear when threatened with the gun, the shooting would never have occurred.

Moreover, Francesco had no previous criminal history, but seemed to be infatuated with his gun. In most circumstances where a person is outnumbered by those who threaten him or her, getting away would be the logical action to take. But here, Francesco appears to suggest that the possession of a firearm directly changed his self-perception to that of a person in control—a person not to be wronged. It is clear that his feared image of a confrontational person who was wronged was not effectively communicated to his victim. Francesco miscued the victim's noncompliance, even after displaying his gun. Like many of the interviewees, Francesco claims he became the threatened party and had to shoot to protect himself.

Denial of Injury

As might be expected, a few inmates justified their gun use by claiming that there was no injury to the victim. These accounts were used mainly by career robbers. Antwan, one of the few career convenience store robbers in the sample, explains his gun use as necessary because it actually prevented people from getting hurt.

ANTWAN: I guess you could say, nobody's going to argue with it [gun], and whatever you want them to do they're going to do.
INTERVIEWER: You never had a problem with people trying to pick up a weapon back at you?
ANTWAN: No.
INTERVIEWER: What if they did? What would you have done? Think.
ANTWAN: I probably would have left.
INTERVIEWER: If they shoot you, you think you would've left without shooting them?

ANTWAN: Yeah, it's pretty hard to say.

INTERVIEWER: You didn't worry about it? Your guns were loaded, I take it?

ANTWAN: Yeah.

INTERVIEWER: Why were they loaded if you weren't going to shoot anybody?

ANTWAN: I don't know, you never know. I would never, you know I said when I did the robberies my intention was for the money, not to hurt anybody. I think I thought, at the time, I had control and would-n't have to do that. I never worried about hurting anybody because I never had that intention. I never went in thinking, "All right, if this person doesn't do what he says, I'll just shoot him."

Thus, robbers like Antwan appear to view guns as tools of the profession that are simply used to gain control of the situation and prevent injury to themselves and others. It is ironic, however, that many times these same inmates later found themselves in situations where they believed they had to use their gun against another person. Consequently, they were forced to shift their account from denial of injury to denial of victim.

Appeal to Higher Loyalties

Inmates often justified their gun use by claiming devotion to another person or group. For them, gun use was tied to issues that were more important than life and law. Their gun use was clearly a result of their higher loyalty to another individual or group. For instance, several inmates said that they used a gun out of loyalty to help a family member get out of a bad situation. They claimed that they had to help or protect their family member no matter what the cost to themselves and their freedom.

In the following account, Marc uses a mixture of denial of victim and appeal to loyalties to explain why he killed his terminally ill wife when her pain became severe and she held him to a promise he had made to her. Marc was in his fifties and recently retired from the armed services when he shot and killed his wife. Marc justifies shooting his wife to alleviate her pain and suffering because she begged him to end her life. Thus, Marc appeals to a higher power—his bond of marriage and commitment to his wife in sickness and in health. Marc points out several times that his wife made him promise to take her life when her illness progressed to the point she no longer wished to live. Marc was married to his wife for 34 years when he shot and killed her.

MARC: One day, my wife said she had enough. We had talked about it for quite a while so, when the time came, she said, "Do it today." My two grown kids didn't understand why I would do anything like that. It was totally off the wall, out of the norm. But you have to do what you have to do. I didn't give her a lot of drugs all at once because I didn't want her to commit suicide. It was my responsibility; it would have been selfish to refuse her. What I did is nobody's business. People don't know the reason why I did it—they just see what is in the newspapers. I wouldn't tell them anything [police, district attorney]. I figured it was between me and my wife. I really felt personally it was none of their business—this is what I felt. I figured I did it and will stand up and do the time [30 years]. I don't suppose there would be anything wrong with telling them why I shot my wife but, at the time, I felt it was a private matter. I felt that, if I told the whole story, that I would have kind of disowned her. I don't feel that I owe anybody any explanation because it was between me and my wife.

Thus, Marc's appeal to higher loyalties as a justification for his actions is clearly apparent. The offense of taking his wife's life in this incident was committed with a handgun his mother-in-law gave him some two years before the shooting of his ill wife. She was getting older and giving her possessions away so he got a handgun her husband had owned years earlier. In this most interesting offense, an ill woman's request to have her life ended placed her husband in a very untenable position. Never did Marc and his wife discuss the legal ramifications of what would happen to him once he committed the offense. Further, everything that occurred from the actual shooting to the judicial proceedings, which resulted in a second-degree murder conviction, was thought to be a private affair between him and his wife. Nowhere does Marc perceive the public consequences of his act. In sum, he continues to emphasize that it is not the state's business, but instead a private agreement between two consenting adults. According to Marc, there was no victim. Neither he nor his dead wife were victims, thus there need be no guilt on his part. He was simply carrying out her wishes after 34 years of marriage. The interviewer probed about what might be considered a more humane way of end-ing one's life by an overdose of lethal drugs but, as noted above, Marc thought that suicide was wrong as compared to shooting his wife with a handgun. It seems there are no gray areas for this particular offender. He knew what was right and he justifies his action by saying that he misses his wife, but feels he did no wrong. It is as if he perceives himself an honorable man for the sacrifices he made as a result of honoring his wife's wishes by fulfilling a sacred promise.

Condemnation of the Condemners

Only a few of our inmates used condemnation of the condemners justification when explaining their gun violence. According to Sykes and Matza (1957), the purpose of condemning the condemners is to shift the focus of the deviance to those who disapprove of the violations. Thus, a few inmates talked about the role of the authorities in facilitating the spread of guns in their neighborhoods, for example, as Ricardo explains.

> RICARDO: I remember one time back in the 1970s when [the US government] brought a railroad car and left it [there]. I knew the project's cats were going to get it. That's because that's what they used to do. What was there were a couple of railroad cars full of guns. Full of guns! And it flooded the Los Angeles community. Guns, we talking .38s, .22s, rifles, and shotguns. They actually left it there . . . on purpose! I remembered this because those guns flooded [my neighborhood]. Now we know who makes the guns, I'm going to have to go to the racial factor here.

Thus, Ricardo points out that much of the gun violence in the communities across the United States was prompted by the government, which helped criminals and gang members get guns. Other inmates also echoed Ricardo's beliefs arguing that law enforcement wanted guns in the community so that gangs would fight and kill each other instead of law enforcement focusing its attention on social problems and the abuse of power.

Sad Tale

Scott and Lyman point out that a sad tale is a justification of an untoward act in terms of a bleak past. Thus, a sad tale is an "arrangement of facts that highlight an extremely dismal past, and thus explain the individual's present state" (1968:52). Contrary to many stereotypes about criminals, sad tales were not used often among the interviewees. Most inmates did not claim that their lives were so difficult that it led them to use a gun in the commission of a violent offense. Still, the following account by Tiffiny, who uses a firearm to shoot her boyfriend, clearly illustrates the sad tale justification (combined with the defeasibility excuse explained below and the denial of the victim justification explained above).

TIFFINY: I was going with my boyfriend who I felt I was totally in love with and I couldn't live without and all those things. He wanted to leave me and we played this game off and on for a month. He'd leave me and then come back. The last time I was like, "I can't take this anymore. I don't want to live anymore. I am going to kill myself." I asked my mom for a gun because Randy, who had lived with us, had saw me at the 7-Eleven, and I am afraid of him. But I want to go out so she handed me the gun and I went out. I told my mom a lie. I wanted the gun to kill myself so I told her a different story. I went out to the country to an open field and I fired the gun to make sure I could because I am scared of guns, always have been. I stopped and said to myself, "I have to know what's wrong with me first. I need to know why he doesn't love me the way he said he did." I got back in the car and I drove to an outdoor party where I knew he was at. I told him I had to talk with him and we went and talked inside. I had put the gun in my jacket pocket after I shot it in the field. We talked for like an hour and we were walking back to the car and he said something, I don't remember what, and I took the gun out and I shot him and I shot myself.

Tiffiny claims she had no premeditated thoughts of harming her boyfriend. She begins her account by referencing her mother's ex-boyfriend who we learned, upon further questioning, was sexually abusive to Tiffiny while he resided with the family. Tiffiny argues that the end of her relationship with her boyfriend was simply too much for her to take. She portrays herself as a person who only meant to harm herself, but presents an excuse of not being responsible for her violent actions toward her boyfriend. The events leading up to the actual shooting of her boyfriend and herself appear vague in description and rather coincidental in nature. She clearly claims she was not aware of her actions at the time of the shooting because she could not even remember what her boyfriend said moments before she shot him. Did his final statement (whatever it was) provoke the murder? Or, was the intention there from the beginning to dramatically take both their lives if Tiffiny was not able to reconcile with her boyfriend? The fact that Tiffiny's boyfriend may have said something that she defined as a rejection in those final moments prior to the shooting seemed to us as an attempt to leave open to interviewer interpretation that her boyfriend deserved to be hurt for what he said. However, this justification of denial is not likely to be effective without Tiffiny's sad tale and appeal to defeasibility.

Tiffiny's accounts for shooting her boyfriend are related in such a way as to justify them in terms of a sad tale and then attempt to excuse her as if the sequence of events prior to the shooting was scripted for her to follow and she had little control after procuring the gun from her mother. The latter is an account that indirectly offers the theme of "this wasn't the real me" who committed such a terrible crime.

Excuses

Excuses are "socially approved vocabularies for mitigating or relieving responsibility when conduct is questioned" (Scott and Lyman 1968:47). Sykes and Matza (1957) identify four excuses that we found to be used by the inmates in this study: defeasibility, scapegoating, accident, and fatalism. The defeasibility excuse was employed most often by inmates to explain their gun use.

Defeasibility

Scott and Lyman (1968) state that appeals to defeasibility are excuses that claim criminal behavior was the result of the lack of knowledge and will. The inmates who used this excuse essentially asserted that they were not completely free at the time they used a firearm. It is interesting to note that inmates' excuses of defeasibility were almost always accompanied by at least one other excuse or justification. The following account illustrates an appeal to defeasibility because Darrel, who shot his stepfather, was not thinking clearly. Moreover, Darrel claims that he was manipulated into the shooting by a close friend who encouraged the violence. It is interesting to note that women were more likely to use appeals to defeasibility, whereas men were more likely to use denial of victim. Finally, we also believe that Darrel presents an appeal to higher loyalties justification because he argues that his obligation to save his mother's life is more important than anything that could happen to him as a result of his crime.

DARREL: My stepfather would break my mom's ribs, break her jaw, break her nose. You know, he never broke anything on me. . . . I was 18, living on my own and I went to visit my mom. She was living in an apartment, but they weren't living together at the time. She had a black eye so I called my stepdad and told him, "I'm a grown man now. You hit her again and I'm coming after you." He said, "If I hit her again, I'll kill her and I'll end up killing you too." About three weeks later, I saw leather indentations where she had been tied up. The morning of my 19th birthday, I went out and shot him. When I decided that there was no alternative but, but to do what I did to my stepdad, that's when I went and got a gun and used it. So it was like a 12-hour period of being angry and the person with me [interviewee's friend] was egging me on. He was having me go through every time I'd seen my stepdad hit my mom and every time he hit me. Every time I started to cool down, he would start in again. So he kept me pumped up ready to do this until the act occurred. I was totally disconnected from myself in the act. Once the act was complete, I saw somebody I didn't know shooting my stepdad. Once the act was over, I'm back to myself, total rush, dizziness, everything was blurry, adrenaline rush, and he's still standing asking me why. I just freaked out.

Darrel suggests that, when he murdered his abusive stepfather, it released his pent-up emotions after years of physical abuse to his mother and himself. Yet he accounts for the decision to shoot his abusive stepfather only after his friend kept reminding him of all the terrible abusive incidents he had experienced over the years. He uses, in part, his friend's persuasiveness to help justify the shooting. True, Darrel's stepfather was a long-time abuser and needed to be stopped. However, Darrel indicates that he may not have shot his abusive stepfather had it not been for his friend's constant reminders of his past beatings at the hands of his stepfather.

Darrel relates the feeling that, after he actually shot the victim, he experienced a disconnection from his physical person and notes that he visualized someone else dong the shooting. This indicates a presentation of self as a person who would not commit such a violent act. It was as if somebody other than himself did the shooting. Darrel's account has the objective of relating the type of person he really is: one whose self-presentation is a nonviolent person who was overwhelmed by his circumstances. Further, Darrel justifies the shooting because of his responsibility to be his mother's protector. By including his mother to help justify his foreground thoughts of killing his stepfather, he offers an almost heroic self-image as the boy who is now a man and therefore must confront the evil abuser. In reality, it is difficult to discern if Darrel was getting even with the victim for his own years of abuse or to rectify the years that his mother had experienced abuse. For Darrel, protecting his mother heightens his image as a guardian of a weak person rather than that of an angry retaliator who is getting back for his own past abuse. The justification for his action, although wrong, is perceived as necessary.

Scapegoating

A few inmates used scapegoating as an excuse to explain their gun violence. Scapegoating is the allegation that criminal behavior is a response to the behavior or attitude of another (Scott and Lyman 1968). The following account by Brandee helps to illustrate this unusual excuse and differentiate it clearly from self-defense accounts that employ denial of victim as a justification. It is important to note that Brandee illustrates both scapegoating and, to some extent, defeasibility as excuses for her violence.

BRANDEE: The boyfriend I had at the time I don't know, we were just kind of having fun. That's how I looked at it. Not that the crimes that we committed were fun or anything. We partied a lot, did drugs and stuff but, more than that, we were just having fun and living it up. Then, in the summer in the period of a couple months, we just went on a robbery spree. . . . It all started while we were watching the movie *Point Break*. He was sitting there saying, "We could do that." I was like, "Oh, yeah, that is a great idea," and it just went on from there. I mean he could not stop talking about it . . . thinking about it. Then, it kinda turned to a manipulation thing. He said, "I am serious about this and I could find another partner, but I really trust you, and if I have to I will." I was in love with this guy and thinking he is not really going to do this with anybody else. We were just being dumb. I don't think we considered that it was really a violent act. We did have a gun and we pulled it on someone when we walked into the store, but it wasn't like we ran in and roared. It was weird. . . . You cannot count how many people will be in the store, who the clerk is, what they are doing, unless you study them and we really didn't. It wasn't like some big planned thing, it was really spontaneous. We didn't know if we were going to do anything until we were there, then after go back to work [summer job] and do it again on another day.

Brandee and her boyfriend committed three armed robberies of large discount department stores in a short period of time. Brandee's boyfriend insisted that she hide at her parents' house the gun that they used during the crimes. After he bragged to a few friends about their criminal acts, one of those friends informed the authorities who, in turn, questioned Brandee's boyfriend about the incidents. He told authorities where to find the gun and then became the state's lead witness against Brandee. For that, he received a court sentence to a drug treatment program while Brandee received a 12-year sentence to prison.

Brandee argues that she participated in these robberies without thinking about the consequences of being involved in serious crime. Of course, she implies that, if she would have thought about the consequences of her actions, she never would have engaged in the robberies. She also explains that her affection for her boyfriend overcame her sensibilities, and contends that she had no choice but to go along with his wishes or possibly lose him. Thus, Brandee claims that her motives were to maintain her romantic relationship. This account might also be viewed as a justification in the sense that it served the interests of another to which she has an "unbreakable allegiance of affection." Brandee implies that she never really thought they would commit the first robbery. However, she subsequently engaged in several armed robberies prior to being apprehended by the police. Here, Hewitt and Stokes's (1975) thematic organization of meaning applies. It is based on interactions, which most often are dependent on people's ability to interpret the actions of others as types of particular identities. When events fail to fit themes in interaction, which appears to be the case here, identities may become problematic if the acts of others do not in reality appear sensible in light of a person's identity in the situation. Maybe Brandee's boyfriend is not who he appeared to be.

The boyfriend's fantasy identity as a "bad guy" was not really who he was. Brandee notes that he escaped any meaningful punishment. Instead, the seriousness of his criminal escapades, as short-lived as they were, forced him to quickly return to a conventional status, And he blamed Brandee (also using the excuse of scapegoating) for his fantasized criminal identity. Brandee did not believe that her boyfriend was serious about his claim to be an outlaw. In the end, however, she was stigmatized with the outlaw label while her boyfriend's account (that he was led astray by Brandee) was accepted and he was sent to drug rehabilitation.

Accident

Only a few offenders argued that shooting their gun was simply an accident and, thus, did not represent who they are. Tim represents one such case. Tim was a small-time methamphetamine dealer with a criminal history who shot his live-in girlfriend by mistake. This claim of accidental harm is also bolstered by an excuse of defeasibility that the shooting was a result of extenuating circumstances. Tim uses the fact that he was sleep deprived and abusing methamphetamine to explain his state of mind when the accidental shooting occurred.

TIM: I was barely out of prison a year when I got laid off from my job. So I chipped a little with speed [meth] and ended up selling it because this is what I do. I carry a gun because you just never know what can happen. So I would pick up the dope and carry my gun. When I was done, I would put the gun away. I was selling to a few customers and I was doing alright. I was working part time at a job, trying to save up to start my own business. I am realizing I am doing too much at once. I am now working long hours working for these people all over the place. At this time, I was living with this lady and her daughter. One day, I go and pick up my weekly shipment of meth and I am carrying my gun. I am very tired, and I pushed myself beyond the limit. I was working 53 days nonstop plus taking meth, and I'm already past paranoia. I need sleep, but I was almost there to get my goal of having enough money to own my own business. So by now I've lost control, but yet I am still able to drive my car. All I had to do is pull in my woman's driveway, walk in the house and get some sleep. I was so tired and high that I fell asleep in the car in her driveway. The sun's coming through the windshield, and I just passed out. I've got my gun there with me. Here comes my girlfriend, her mom, and sister out of the house. They see me sleeping in my car, and they try and wake me up. My car door is already opened. I wake up and pull the gun and shoot because I think it's somebody who wants my drugs, and I shoot somebody I love. I'm here 14 years already for that. She didn't die, but she got a pretty good chunk of her liver taken out where the bullet went. I guess most of what happened was because I didn't think I was ever sober enough to ever really know that I was on this wreck until it was too late.

Tim blames his frequent use of methamphetamine, which led to a lack of sleep and paranoia, and his fear that someone was stealing his drugs for the shooting. Tim makes it clear to us that the shooting was indeed an accident because no one would shoot someone they loved. For this incident, Tim also blames too many days of legitimate employment supplemented by the illegal sale of meth, all for the purpose of having enough capital to start his own business. Thus, he additionally appeals to notions of defeasibility—he was not really free to pursue legitimate business ventures. Tim never mentions what type of business he intended to start. Was his goal of becoming a business owner just another excuse to take and sell drugs, or was it a legitimate goal? That question remains unanswered.

Fatalism

Fatalism as an excuse is drawn from the notion that biological or cultural forces (rather than free will choices) drive deviant behavior (Sykes and Matza 1957). Thus, the outcome is predetermined or certain. Giselle, a female gang leader, uses a fatalistic excuse to argue that she was going to have to shoot someone sooner or later because she was a gang member—something many of our gang members stated. For Giselle, it was just a matter of time. Giselle also argues that the victim deserved to be shot (i.e., denial of victim). Giselle claims that she had a reputation to uphold as being tough and courageous. She notes that her leadership in an all-female gang was well known because of her reputation as a fighter. She was fatalistic in her tale because she argued that being a gang member dictates that you will be constantly challenged by other gang members. Giselle told us about several instances where she felt that she was bound to use a gun. The following account discusses her excuse for using her gun to shoot the challenger.

GISELLE: I always had a weapon, firearm. I think I felt firearms are safer than a blade, knife. Safer, if I get into it, safer for somebody else. Just because I know when you have a gun, you have to use it and that keeps me from getting involved in a fight. For a year or more, I was harassed by somebody that really didn't know me or shared any kind of thing. But I had a reputation, I had my name out there. I get tested a lot, everywhere I go—in here [prison] as well. I been here incarcerated for six years now. And I've gotten into every kind of quarrel you can imagine, but I've managed. Anyway, it was a female with some more people involved. I had an enemy. She was always coming around. The enemy I had [rival gang member] didn't know why I was on probation, didn't know I had a baby, probably didn't know half the things I was into. And she was drinking, getting high, all the stuff I used to do. She had a bottle for a weapon and another person that was there stopped her from hitting me with it. We were going to fight, but we couldn't do it there because there was a big scene and we just happened to meet up on the street. We both agreed to fight. However, we just started fighting and I got rid of my weapon. She didn't get rid of the bottle. She decided to come at me with it. I picked up my weapon and we were struggling, and the shot went off and that's what happened. The girl got shot, but didn't die. I got 24 years for it—attempted murder and first-degree assault. After I shot her, I felt like I was having a dream. It was all smoky. I couldn't see anything and I left.

Shooting another female gang member during a street fight was something that Giselle claims she had to do and would end up doing sooner or later. Her reputation as a fighter who had never lost was on the line. Although she explains that carrying a handgun prevented her from getting into physical altercations with rivals, she ended up using it to shoot her challenger because her rival refused to give up her weapon and "fight fair." Not wishing to fight this challenger because of her probation status and being a parent are some indications that Giselle is a changed person. Nevertheless, she allows the group of onlookers to place her in a position to not back down. The result is that Giselle shoots her aggressor because she is attacked with a bottle (denial of victim justification). Giselle explains that she had been involved in many criminal activities, but had outgrown her involvement with this type of life, largely due to having a baby and an understanding probation officer. Yet when challenged by another to a fight, she accounts for her participation in the physical encounter by explaining how this gang rival had harassed her in the past and confronted her in front of a group of her peers. Giselle's well-earned reputation was being publicly challenged and, according to her story, she had no choice but to fight. By relating her predicament in such a myopic format, Giselle allows her account of the shooting to be an untenable situation by being placed in a conflicting circumstance, one in which she claims that she had no choice but to do what she did. In this instance, her mitigating explanation permits her to cloud her perception of the shooting by alleviating any responsibility for what occurred.

The Complexity of Accounts

We found that a majority of inmates drew upon many accounts and justifications when telling us their stories. These accounts usually blended together several types of excuses and justifications, and often relied, at least to some extent, on the more common appeals to defeasibility and denial of victim. Thus, the complexity of accounts made a primary account hard to identify. These are, in a word, not the ideal types of accounts that are explored by Sykes and Matza (1957). As an illustration of this important point, we examine the account that Edwin uses to explain why he shot and killed his victim. Edwin was clearly comfortable with guns, having used them several times to intimidate people in past situations when he was involved in disagreements. Edwin is a white middle-aged suburban resident who was, at the time of his offense, a small businessman who had recently declared bankruptcy. The violent incident in question involves the repossession of his truck by the bank that loaned him the money to purchase it. Edwin's account for his behavior falls into both excuses and justifications as demonstrated by his story of the event that led up to his murdering the contracted bank repossession truck driver.

EDWIN: I developed some personal liability and, once bankruptcy was declared, they came to repossess a truck which was registered to the business. I had a verbal agreement with my banker that would take over the payments personally so he wouldn't have to eat it. I had been reassured by my attorney numerous times that they wouldn't mess with the vehicles or the house. One night at 3 o'clock in the morning, I heard my truck start, and I thought I would be John Wayne and run downstairs and stop it from being stolen. I took my gun and let off a couple of shots, and I hit him in the right eye and killed him. I wouldn't do it again for all the tea in China, and wasn't trying to do it then, but he was still dead and that's what got me here [prison]. I was anything but a complete whole human being when I was out there. I was an idiot. I had no value system. I had no goals. I lived from the belief of a saying on a bumper sticker, "He who dies with the most toys wins." And I was going to have the most toys, one way or another. I always stayed within the lines of the law, but ethics and morals were out the window. I cheated on my wife, and my ego was all that mattered to me. I couldn't feed my ego enough. It was the same as if I was on heroin. I would pick a fight, buy something, or acquire some new property or a new girlfriend and, as soon as I did that, I would feel guilty and ashamed and need another fix. I know that what made me feel good was women and toys. There was no sane reason to go running out there the way I did and shoot at the repo guy. It was all about me needing to prove myself. I can do this. I can handle this. You're not going to do this to me. I know in my heart of hearts that I sure never intended to kill anybody. I have never even given it a thought that it's better to kill people than hurt them. I intended to shoot a couple of shots at him and that will scare him off. I heard the truck start, jump up, look at the window, turn around, grab my gun, and run outside. It couldn't have lasted a minute and a half, personally less than one minute from me waking up and him being dead.

For me, my dispute with the man who I killed started years before I met up with him. I learned to solve problems by overpowering people. When you can't overpower with money, you talk louder. And if you can't talk louder and intimidate them, then maybe you shock them. And if you can't shock them, you can show them a gun and scare them. Maybe you pop a couple of rounds off in the air, you know, then it just escalates. That thought process is what causes me to take a gun and run outside and pop a couple of shots off. And then, sadly, that is what ended up killing him.

According to Edwin, shooting the man who came to repossess his truck appears to be rationalized in the form of a justification when he claims his agreement with the bank allowed him to continue to make payments after his business was legally declared bankrupt. However, after a more detailed reading of this account, Edwin seems to be saying that he was not aware that the bank would be taking his truck and, if had he been fully informed of the bank's intention, the murder would not have occurred. That is, Edwin is using a defeasibility account of the situation. He indicates that there was a mistake made by the bank. Edwin's attorney had assured him that his home and truck were safe from repossession. He argues to us that the shooting occurred only because the man was repossessing his vehicle at 3:00 A.M.

Edwin's continued account for shooting and killing the victim in this deadly encounter is one of insight by hindsight. He relates a lengthy tale of his past life that led up to the shooting. He tells of his past attitudes and the way he treated people, and his current realization of what he once was, but is not now. He appeals to mitigate his past actions toward people by explaining (defeasibility excuse) that all of his past behavioral history was formed long before the shooting. The shooting would have happened sooner or later (fatalistic), but it just happened to be the repossession incident that set him off. Interestingly, in his last statement describing what occurred that tragic night, Edwin indicates that it was his "thought process" that caused the killing, not actually him. It was the shots that he intended to fire in the air that "accidentally" killed the repossession man. This allows Edwin to disassociate himself from committing the actual murder. Lastly, Edwin spends a great deal of time discussing his acquired insight for his violent activity, but never mentions the harm that was done to the victim or his family. There is no doubt that Edwin feels remorse for what happened, but one gets the impression that he may be feeling more sorry for the consequences that he is experiencing than for the victim.

Discussion

We present this study's findings in the form of narratives that are meant to provide insight into the types of accounts the inmates offer for their gun-related violence. The narratives that we chose to include in this analysis are rich in description and representative of the ideal types of accounts given by inmates. We focus largely on the various accounts that deny the victim because that was commonly used by the interviewees to explain their behavior. The narratives provided are accurate in that they depict a broad illustration of accounts. To further clarify the frequency of accounts, Figure 2.1 shows the accounts used by the inmates in the sample. Keep in mind that many inmates used more than one account to explain their gun violence.

As Figure 2.1 suggests, accounts of gun-related violence fall mainly into two groups as explained above: justifications and excuses. Again, the most common justification used by the inmates in the sample is denial of victim. When inmates use the denial of victim justification, they imply that their victim deserved the injury (Sykes and Matza 1957). Inmates also offered excuses as explanations of criminal acts. Specifically, and as Figure 2.1 illustrates, many inmates presented accounts that used the excuse of defeasibility to explain their gun violence. As demonstrated above, defeasibility was rarely used as the only account for gun violence. In other words, defeasibility was often used as an excuse, but was used together with other excuses, justifications, or both.

Figure 2.1 also indicates that a few inmates offered no account of their behavior. In effect, they were telling us that the act represented

Figure 2.1 Excuses and Justifications Used by Inmates to Account for Their Gun Violence

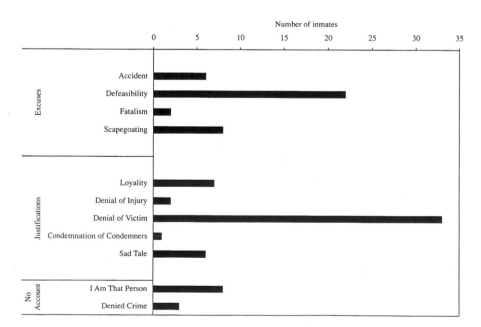

who they really were. In most instances, these inmates were robbers or gang members. A gun was simply part of their occupation and identity. We often had a difficult time distinguishing between these few instances where no account was offered and the potential fatalistic excuse. Were these just poor attempts at offering up an account? We also should point out that three inmates plainly denied that they had committed a gun crime even though they had been convicted of the offense.

The consequences of deviant activity are often dependent on a given "definition of the situation." When a definition of a specific situation emerges, even though its dominance may be only temporary, individuals must adjust their behavior and views to it. Goffman (1974) explains this behavior as "framing." If a problematic interpretation of an interviewee's behavior was called into question, he or she was likely to refocus our attention on alternative explanations of that behavior. When these alternative definitions of problematic situations would arise, they were subject to negotiation. Thus, it is incumbent on convicted offenders to have their situation defined in ways most favorable to maintaining or advancing their own interests. When "transformations of identity" are at stake, such efforts become especially consequential (Strauss 1962:63). The rejection of a deviant identity has ramifications for that person's self-perception of who they are. As noted earlier, the negotiation of accounts is really a negotiation of identities. Accounts serve as a management technique, or "front," that minimizes the threat to identity (Goffman 1967). If a violent perpetrator can offer an acceptable account for his or her violent gun use, he or she increases the likelihood of restoring a conventional identity brought into question by the criminal behavior.

There is a close link between successfully conveying desired images to others and being made to incorporate them in one's own self-construction. When individuals offer accounts for their problematic actions, they are trying to ease their situation in two ways: (1) by convincing others and (2) by convincing themselves. An important function of accounts is to make an individual's transgressions intelligible to themselves and others. The gun users we interviewed sought to dispel the view that their deviation was a defining characteristic of who they really were. In short, they attempted to engage the centrality or primacy of a deviant role imputation. To accomplish this task, they offered accounts that were primarily focused on the denial of victim and a combination of justifications and excuses that surrounded the excuse of defeasibility. Goffman (1967) would argue that the goal of the inmates in this study was to maintain or restore their own sense of personal worth notwithstanding their violent behavior. In a way, laying claim to a favorable image in spite of aberrant behavior also means voiding an apparent moral reality that is obvious to the deviant.

Individuals seek a "common ground" in accounts of their deviant behavior, explaining their actions in conventional terms that are acceptable to a particular audience. Inmate accounts often relied on several types of excuses and justifications to explain their gun violence. Thus, Sykes and Matza's (1957) ideal types were uncommon in our data. Nonetheless, it is important to point out that these accounts should not be viewed as mere rationalizations. It appeared to us that these gun offenders truly believed in their accounts. Moreover, accounts do not themselves prove the cause of one's behavior. They do, however, provide contextually specific answers about the act in question and manifest a certain style of looking at the world.

Finally, it should be noted that, as retrospective interpretations, accounts often have little to do with the motives that existed at the time the violent act occurred. In this case, accounting for deviant behavior requires one to dissimulate; that is, to pretend to be what one is not or not to be what one is. Thus, it is not logically necessary to agree with another's moral judgments to employ accounts. Even where no guilt or shame is consciously felt, a person may offer accounts in the hope of lessening what even so could be attributions of a deviant identity. In Chapter 3, we examine the source of the justifications and excuses for a specific group of the inmates in this study whose gun violence is tied to their common material circumstances. Specifically, we examine how guns and accounts of gun use are influenced by street gang culture.

3

Guns and
Street Gang Culture

M ANY OF THE INMATES WHO WE INTERVIEWED WERE EXTEN-
sively involved in street gangs. We found that guns were central
to street gang culture and activity (see Hagedorn and Davis 2008). In
this chapter, we focus on the way that gangs promote violent gun use.
We argue that socialization is important because it helps to shape a
gang member's identity and sense of self. Moreover, guns often help
gang members project their violent identities. As Kubrin argues, "the
gun becomes a symbol of power and a remedy for disputes"
(2005:363). Prior to our analysis of gang members, we briefly review
the literature on the relationship between gangs, crime, guns, and violence. In that review, we emphasize the importance of socialization
and the impact of gangs on identity and self. We provide some insight
into how guns may help gang members shape and convey their identity. Finally, in our discussion, we relate the findings to the relative
efficacy of different intervention strategies that are focused on reducing gang violence.

Gangs and Violence

Research suggests that gang members are more likely than nongang
members to engage in crime, especially violent crime (Gordon et al.
2004). According to Thornberry and colleagues, the relationship

between gang affiliation and violence "is remarkably robust, being reported in virtually all American studies of gang behavior regardless of when, where, or how the data were collected" (1993:75). Although the relationship between gangs and violence is pervasive, "little is known about the causal mechanisms that bring it about" (Thornberry et al. 1993:76). Do gangs attract individuals who are predisposed to violence, or do they create violent individuals? The debate in the literature about these explanations of gang violence is rather extensive.

Thornberry and colleagues (1993) point out that there are three perspectives that inform the debate concerning the relationship between gangs and violence. First, the selection perspective argues that gang members are individuals who are delinquent and violent prior to joining the gang. Thus, gang members are individuals who are likely to engage in violent and deviant behavior even if they are not gang members (Gerrard 1964; Yablonsky 1962). From this perspective, what makes gang members more criminal is that more criminal individuals have self-selected or been recruited into gangs. The second perspective is known as the social facilitation perspective. This perspective argues that gang members are no different from nongang members until they enter the gang. Therefore, the gang serves a normative function. Briefly, the gang is the source of delinquent behavior because new gang members are socialized into the norms and values of gang life, which provides the necessary social setting for crime and violence to flourish. Thornberry and colleagues (1993) note that the third explanation of the relationship between gangs and crime is the enhancement perspective. The enhancement perspective proposes that new gang members are recruited from a pool of individuals who show propensity to engage in crime and violence, but their level of violence intensifies once they enter the gang because the gang provides a structure that encourages crime and violence (see also Decker and Van Winkle 1996).

According to McCorkle and Miethe, the second and third explanations for gang-related crime are the most popular explanations in the literature because both perspectives rely on the assumption that social disorganization increases socialization into the gang subculture, which produces crime (2002:111). Recent criminological research suggests that the enhancement perspective is the most likely explanation for the association between gang involvement and criminal behavior. For instance, Gordon and colleagues (2004) discovered that individuals who join gangs are, in general, more delinquent than their peers before they join the gang. However, Gordon and colleagues also found that violent behavior among individuals who join a gang significantly increases after they become a gang member. Although Gordon and colleagues' work provides some answers concerning the potential causal mechanisms of gang violence, it leaves open the question about why gang members increase their violent behavior after they join a gang. It is for that reason that we focus this research on the concept of socialization as a mechanism that leads to gang-related gun violence.

Gang Socialization

Research on *gang socialization*, which is the process of learning the appropriate values and norms of the gang culture to which one belongs, suggests that group processes are highly important (Miller and Brunson 2000; Sirpal 1997; Vigil 1988). In addition, Moore (1991) believes that many city gangs have become quasi-institutionalized. In these cities, gangs have played a major role in ordering individuals' lives at the same time that other important social institutions such as schools and families have played less of a normative role (see also Bjerregaard and Lizotte 1995; Blumstein 1995a; Dowker and Klein 1983; Vigil 1988). Vigil finds that gangs help to socialize "members to internalize and adhere to alternative norms and modes of behavior and play a significant role in helping . . . youth acquire a sense of importance, self-esteem, and identity" (1988:63). One alternative norm used to attain status is to develop a reputation for being violent (Anderson 1999). This reputation for violence, however, is likely to develop, at least to some degree, after an individual joins a gang.

The reasons that individuals join gangs are diverse (Decker and Van Winkle 1996). According to Decker and Van Winkle, the most instrumental reason for joining a gang is protection. In addition to instrumental concerns, a large portion of gang members indicate that the gang to which they belong fulfills a variety of more typical adolescent needs, especially companionship and support that tend to be more expressive in nature. That is, the gang is a primary group. The idea that the gang is a primary group into which individuals are socialized is not new. For instance, Thrasher pointed out:

> [The gang] offers the underprivileged boy probably his best opportunity to acquire status and hence it plays an essential part in the development of his personality. In striving to realize the role he hopes to take he may assume a tough pose, commit feats of daring or vandalism, or become a criminal. (1927:230)

Thus, gang violence may often be viewed as expressive in nature. The value of masculinity as a form of expression plays an important role in gang socialization (Miller and Decker 2001). Oliver (1994) argues that gang violence is often a method of expressing one's masculinity when opportunities to pursue conventional roles are denied. Acts of manhood, note Decker and Van Winkle, are "important values of [a member's] world and their psyches—to be upheld even at the cost of their own or others' lives" (1996:186). Katz (1988) also believes violence plays an important and acceptable role in the subculture of people living in socially isolated environments and economically deprived areas because violence provides a means for a gang member to demonstrate his toughness, and displays of violent retaliation establish acceptance within the gang.

According to Short and Strodtbeck (1965; see also Howell 1998), a good portion of all gang violence can be attributed to threats to one's status within the gang. Gang membership therefore helps to create within-group identity that defines how group members perceive people outside their formal organizational structure. By way of altercasting (i.e., the use of tactics to create identities and roles for others), gangs cast nonmembers into situated roles and identities that are to the gang's advantage (Weinstein and Deutschberger 1963). Altercasting is an aggressive tactic that gangs often use to justify their perception of other gangs as potentially threatening rivals and to rationalize the use of physical violence against other gangs. If the objective of a gang is to be perceived by the community, rival gangs, law enforcement officials, and others in a particular way, then their collective group and individual identities will be located in these defining situations. Even though there is a good deal of research examining the important relationship between violence and status within the gang as it relates to socialization, little is known about the specific ways that status impacts gang violence.

Socialization into the gang is bound up in issues of identity and self. Identity, according to Stone (1962), is the perceived social location of the person. Image, status, and a host of other factors that affect identity are mostly created by group perceptions of who we are and how we define ourselves. "People see themselves from the standpoints of their group and appropriate action in relation to those groups becomes a source of pride" (Shibutani 1961:436). Berger states that "identities are socially bestowed, socially maintained, and socially transformed" (1963:92).

Moore suggests that "the gang represents a means to what is an expressive, rather than an instrumental, goal: the acting out of a male role of competence and of 'being in command' of things" (1978:60). The findings of Decker and Van Winkle (1996) and Moore (1978) suggest that, although instrumental reasons for joining a gang are important, members see the gang largely as an important primary group that is central to their lives and that heavily influences their identity and personality. As a primary group, the approval of gang peers is highly important. It is this expressive reason for remaining in a gang that may help to explain gang crime and violence, especially as it relates to socialization. Hughes and Short (2005) provide insight into the area of identity and gang violence. Specifically, they find that, when a gang member's identity is challenged, violence is often a result, especially if the challenger is a stranger. If a gang member does not comply with gang role expectations when they are challenged, the result may be a loss of respect. Thus, it is important to project a violent reputation to command respect and deter future assaults. Walking away from conflict is risky to a gang member's health (Anderson 1999). By necessity, gang members must make efforts to show a continued commitment to role expectations to the group (Lindesmith and Strauss 1968). From this perspective, it appears that character traits that are a consequence of being socialized into street gangs may result in youthful acts of violence through transformations in identity (Vigil 1996).

Initiation rites are one important aspect of identity formation (Hewitt 1988; Vigil 1996). New gang members are obligated to go through initiation rites that demonstrate commitment to the gang and attest to the individual's desire to gain official membership in the organization. Hewitt (1988) argues that these types of acts help create a "situated self," where a person's self can be defined and shaped by particular situations. Thus, notions of identity formation are highly consistent with notions of gang violence as a function of social facilitation and enhancement perspectives in that they explain why gang members may increase their levels of crime and violence once they join the gang. Moreover, research suggests that the more significant the relationship to a gang is, the more committed an individual is to a gang identity (Callero 1985; Stryker and Serpe 1982). In sum, gangs provide a reference group for expected role behavior and shape a member's identity and sense of self (Callero 1985). The greater a member's commitment to a gang identity, the more frequently he or she will perform in ways that enact that identity, which include acts of violence (Stryker and Serpe 1982).

Guns also play an important role in many gangs, and are often reported to be owned for instrumental reasons (Decker and Van Winkle 1996). For instance, Lizotte and colleagues (1994) argue that guns are perceived to be necessary for protection. Gang members who sense a threat from rival gangs are believed to carry guns to protect themselves and their neighborhoods (Decker and Van Winkle 1996; Horowitz 1983; Lizotte et al. 1994; Wright and Rossi 1986). Gang membership "strongly and significantly increases the likelihood of carrying a gun" (Thornberry et al. 2003:131). However, the reason that gang members carry guns remains unclear. It is likely that, in addition to instrumental reasons for carrying a gun, gang members also carry guns for expressive reasons (Sheley and Wright 1995). That is, guns provide gang members with a sense of power that may be extremely important in identity formation. Guns help gang members project a tough image. Thornberry and colleagues report that gang members who carry guns may feel "emboldened to initiate criminal acts that they may otherwise avoid" (2003:125).

Sociologists have long recognized that symbols are important indicators of identity. This is especially true of gangs (Decker and Van Winkle 1996; Vigil 2003). Gang members often display symbols of gang membership, and this is part of being socialized into the role of a gang member.

> Wearing gang clothes, flashing gang signs, and affecting other outward signs of gang behavior are also ways to become encapsulated in the role of gang member, especially through the perceptions of others, who, when they see the external symbols of membership respond as if the person was a member. (Decker and Van Winkle 1996:75)

Bjerregaard and Lizotte argue that it is plausible that "juveniles are socialized into the gun culture by virtue of their gang membership and activity" (1995:42). Although there is some indication that gang members are more likely to own guns than nongang members prior to joining a gang, gang membership also clearly appears to increase the prevalence of gun ownership. Bjerregaard and Lizotte believe that future research needs to focus on why gang membership encourages gun ownership. In this vein, Sanders's (1994) research on drive-by shootings provides some insight into why gang membership may encourage gun ownership. Drawing from Goffman's (1961a) notion of realized resources, Sanders argues that gangs are organizations that provide the necessary context for drive-bys. Sanders is clear when he states that guns and cars are the least important resources in producing drive-bys. However, it is also true that guns are necessary for drive-bys to occur and, as such, are an important part of gang culture to the extent that drive-bys help gang members "build an identity as having heart" (Sanders 1994:204). Thus, notions of character and identity provide a way to look at drive-by shootings as a product of the gang structure where guns are important instruments in building identity. Given the importance of guns to a gang member's identity, it is interesting to note that little research exists that examines the relationship between guns and gangs in terms of identity formation.

Findings

We divide the findings into four sections. First, we focus on the interviewees' socialization into the gang and the impact that socialization has on their self and identity. Second, we explore the importance of gang commitment as reinforcing a gang member's self and identity. Third, we focus on masculinity as a central value among gang members. During discussions of masculinity in the interviews, gang members often referred to the notions of respect and reputation. Reputation is a way that gang members can project their image of masculinity to others. Respect was often referenced when their masculine identity was challenged. Finally, we focus on the importance of guns as instruments central to the lives of the interviewed gang members in the sense that they help project and protect masculine identities.

Gang Socialization, Self, and Identity

Goffman argues that, as individuals, we are often "taken in by our own act" and therefore begin to feel like the person we are portraying (1959:17). Baumeister and Tice (1984) describe this process as one where initial behaviors are internalized so that they become part of a person's self-perception. Once initial behaviors are internalized, the individual continues to behave in ways consistent with his or her self-perception. Related to this study, the socialization process of becoming a gang member required a change in the interviewee's self-perception. That is, who did these gang members become as compared to who they once were? Social interaction is highly important in the process of socialization because it helps create one's identity and sense of self, as Holstein and Gubrium point out.

> As personal as they seem, our selves and identities are extremely social. They are hallmarks of our inner lives, yet they take shape in relation to others. We establish who and what we are through social interaction. In some respects, selves and identities are two sides of the same coin. Selves are the subjects we take ourselves to be; identities are the shared labels we give to these selves. We come to know ourselves in terms of the categories that are socially available to us. (2003:119)

Most inmates who we interviewed appeared to indicate that their socialization into the gang began at a relatively young age. For example, Sidney argues that he started gangbanging early.

SIDNEY: At about 15, I started getting affiliated with the Crips. I knew all these guys, grew up with them, and they were there. . . . I mean, it was like an influence at that age. I met this dude named Bob from Los Angeles at that time. He was a Crip, and he showed me a big wad of money. He said, "Hey man, you want some of this?" "Like yeah! God damn straight. You know I want some of that." He showed me how to sell crack and so, at 15, I went from being scared of the police and respecting them to hustling and selling crack. Now, I'm affiliated with the Crips; I mean it was just unbelievable.

Miquel tells of his orientation in becoming a member of a gang. He points out the glamour that he associated with membership at an impressionable age.

MIQUEL: I started gangbanging when I was 10. I got into a gang when I was 13. I started just hanging around them, just basically idolizing them. I was basically looking for a role model for my generation and ethnic background. The main focus for us is the popularity that they got. That's who the kids looked up to. They had status, better clothes, and better lifestyle.

When Wiley, one of the black interviewees, resided with his father in a mostly white suburban community, he felt estranged from the minority friends that he had in his former neighborhood. Wiley discussed his need to be among his former peers and that he voluntarily moved back to his old neighborhood, "A lot of the people that lived where my father was staying were predominantly white. I mean, not to say I didn't get along with white kids but, you know, it was just two different backgrounds and things of that nature." Wiley's racial and socioeconomic identification in the white community offered little opportunity for him to fit in. When he returned to the city, he quite rapidly became involved with a gang and, according to Wiley, "started getting charged with assaults. Gang rivalry, you know, fighting, just being in a gang." Because he was better educated and did not use street vernacular as his peers did, Wiley claims that he had to continually prove his racial proclivity to his peers.

WILEY: Other kids would call me "white wash" because I spoke proper English. Basically, I wanted to be somebody, so I started hanging around with gangbangers. I was planning on being the best gang member I can be or the best kind of criminal I can be or something like that.

Consistent with Goffman's (1959) observations, once the gang members we studied became active members of a gang, their transformation of identity was complete. That is, consistent with the notion of social facilitation and enhancement perspectives (Thornberry et al. 1993), the self-perceptions and identity of the gang members in this study appear to have changed from what they were prior to joining the gang. Shibutani explains such changes by claiming that "a person's self-perception is caused by a psychological reorientation in which an individual visualizes his world and who he thinks he is in a different light. He retains many of his idiosyncrasies, but develops a new set of values and different criteria of judgment" (1961:523). Violent behavior appeared to play an important role in this transformation of identity and self. Most gang members noted that they engaged in violent behavior more frequently after they joined the gang.

DAVID: At an early age, it was encouraged that I showed my loyalty and do a drive-by . . . anybody they [gangster disciples] deemed to be a rival of the gang. I was going on 14. At first, I was scared to and then they sent me out with one person and I seen him do it. I saw him shoot the guy. . . . So in the middle of a gang fight, I get pulled aside and get handed a pistol. And he said "it's your turn to prove yourself." So I turned around and shot and hit one of the guys [rival gang members]. After that, it just got more easier. I did more and more. I had no concern for anybody.

A further illustration of situated identity and transformation of self is related by another inmate who expresses the person he became through the use of violence and gun possession. Retrospectively, Miquel indicates disbelief in what he had become.

MIQUEL: As a gangbanger, you have no remorse. So basically, they're natural born killers. They are killers from the start. When I first shot my gun for the first time at somebody, I felt bad. It was like, I can't believe I did this. But I looked at my friend and he didn't care at all. Most gangbangers can't have a conscience. You can't have remorse. You can't have any values. Otherwise, you are gonna end up retiring as a gangbanger at a young age.

The situations a person finds themself in, in this case collective gang violence, together with becoming a person who is willing to use violence to maintain membership in the gang, is indicative of a transformed identity. Strauss (1962) claims that, when a person's identity is transformed, they are seen by others as being different than they were before. The individual's prior identity is retrospectively reevaluated in comparison to the present definition of a gang member. Such a transformation was part of the processional change in identity that gang members in this study experienced.

Commitment to the Gang

"As a creature of ideas, man's main concern is to maintain a tentative hold on these idealized conceptions of himself, to legitimate his role identities" (McCall and Simmons 1966:71). Commitment to the gang also serves individual needs for its members. We found that gang identification and loyalty to the group were high priorities for the gang members who we interviewed. This loyalty to the gang was extreme. The interviewees said that they were willing to risk being killed and were committed to taking the life of a rival gang member if the situation called for such action. That is, gang membership helped these interviewees nourish their identity and, at the same time, provided group maintenance (Kanter 1972). As Kanter (1972) points out, the group is an extension of the individual and the individual is an extension of the group. This notion of sacrifice for the group by proving one's gang identification is expressed by Elton's perception of his loyalty.

ELTON: What I might do for my friends [gang peers], you might not do. You've got people out there taking bullets for their friends and killing people. But I'm sure not one of you would be willing to go to that extreme. These are just the thinking patterns we had growing up where I did.

Claude tells about his high degree of identity for his gang, "If you're not a gang member, you're not on my level . . , most of my life revolves around gangs and gang violence. I don't know anything else but gang violence. I was born into it, so it's my life."

The gang members in this study consistently expressed the view that the gang was the most important primary group in a member's life. They often stated that they were willing to kill or be killed for the gang to sustain their self-perception as a loyal gang member. This extreme degree of group affiliation is similar to that shown in activities of the armed services during wartime. The platoon or, in this case the local gang, is worth dying for. In this sense, the notion of the gang as a protector was an important part of gang life for the interviewed gang members. All members were expected to be committed enough to aid their peers should the need arise. Len, a gang member, points to the important role his gang played for him in providing physical safety as well as an assurance of understanding, "That's how it is in the hood, selling dope, gangbangin'. Everybody wants a piece of you—all the rival gang members, all the cops, everybody. The only ones on your side are the gang members you hang with." Len's gang peers are the only people who he perceives will aid him when threatened by others. The world appears full of conflicting situations and, although his gang affiliation is largely responsible for all the groups that are out to harm him in some way, Len nevertheless believes his fellow gang members are the only people who he can depend on.

Violence against rival gangs was a general subject that a majority of the interviewed gang members discussed freely. However, only a few of the violent gang members focused on this subject in comparison to those who were less violence prone. The violent gang members perceived other gangs as ongoing enemies who constantly presented a threat to their safety. As the literature review suggests, there is some debate about whether gang members would be violent without belonging to a gang, or if formal membership in the group provides them with the opportunity to act out this way. However, we find clarity in the inmate accounts in that a gang member's identity provided the context necessary to resort to violence when confronted with conflicting events as did Claude.

CLAUDE: I have hate toward the Crips gang members and have always had hate toward them 'cuz of what they did to my homeboys. . . . I never look back. I do my thing. I always carry a gun no matter what. I am a gang member, man! There are a lot of gang members out to get me for what I done. I shot over 40 people at least. That's what I do.

This perception of being a person who is comfortable with violence and the perception of himself as an enforcer type characterize the role that Claude has played in the past within his gang. Turner (1978) suggests that roles consistent with an individual's self-concept are played more frequently and with a higher degree of participation than roles that are not in keeping with that individual's self-concept. In this situation, Claude nicely fits Turner's explanation of role identity. His hatred for rival gangs and his willingness for retaliation most likely led to his incarceration for attempted murder.

Masculinity, Reputation, and Respect

For the gang members who we interviewed, socialization into the gang and commitment to the gang appear to be central to the notion of masculinity. That is, all interviewed gang members spoke about the importance of masculinity and how it was projected (through the creation of a reputation) and protected (through demands for respect). The notion of masculinity was constantly invoked in relation to self and identity. Thus, masculinity is used to communicate to others what the gang represents and it is used to send an important signal to others who may wish to challenge a gang's collective identity. A gang member's masculine reputation precedes him, so to speak. On an individual level, similar attributes also apply.

> Whatever an individual does and however he appears, he knowing-
> ly and unknowingly makes information available concerning the
> attributes that might be imputed to him and hence the categories in
> which he might be placed. . . . The physical milieu itself conveys
> implications concerning the identity of those who are in it.
> (Goffman 1961a:102)

According to Sherif and Wilson (1953), people's ego attitudes define
and regulate their behavior toward various other groups and are
formed in concert to the values and norms of that person's reference
group. They formulate an important part of their self-identity and
sense of group identification. For the gang members in this study, the
attributes valued by the gangs consisted of factors that projected a
street image, which was necessary to sustain. It was a survival strategy.

Masculinity. Charlie notes that "every man [in a gang] is treated as a
man until proven different. We see you as a man before anything."
Charlie's comment infers the importance of masculinity that his gang
defined as a highly valued attribute among its members. The idea of
manhood and its personal meanings for each interviewee was a subject consistently repeated by all gang members. It usually was
brought up in the context of physical violence, often describing situations where the interviewee had to face danger as a result of another's
threatening behavior or testing of his willingness to use physical
force when insulted by someone outside of the group.

REINALDO: Even if you weren't in one [gang], you got people that
are going to push the issue. We decide what we want to do. I ain't no
punk, I ain't no busta. But it comes down to pride. It's foolish pride,
but a man is going to be a man, and a boy knows he's going to come
into his manhood by standing his ground.

Establishing a reputation coincides with becoming a man, enter-
ing the realm of violence, and being a stand-up guy who will be willing to prove his courage as a true gang member. This strong association between a willingness to perpetrate violence on a considered
rival, or anyone for that matter, was a theme that defined a gang
member's manhood. After eight years in the gang, Jan was owed
money for selling someone dope. After a few weeks of being put off
by the debtor, he had to take some action to appease his gang peers
who were pressuring him to retaliate.

63

JAN: I joined the gang when I was 11 years old. So now that I'm in the gang for eight years, people are asking, "What are you going to do? You got to make a name for yourself." So we went over there [victim's residence] and they were all standing outside and I just shot him. Everybody was happy for me, like "Yea, you shot him, you're cool," and this and that.

A sense of bravado, when displayed, played a utilitarian role in conflicting situations where a gang member attempts to get others to comply with his demands by instilling fear instead of actually utilizing violent means. Having some prior knowledge of the threatening gang member's reputation is helpful in preventing a physical encounter, which is always risky for both parties involved. Again, the importance of firearms in this situation is critical as Wiley emphasizes.

WILEY: The intimidation factor with a gun is amazing. Everybody knows what a gun can do. If you have a certain type of personality, that only increases their fear of you. When it came to certain individuals who I felt were a threat, I would lift my shirt up so they would know I had one on me.

Wiley explains that his firearm served the purpose of avoiding any altercation that could have led to injury or even worse. In these instances, carrying a gun and displaying it proved to be an intimidating, preventative factor for this gang member. The opposite behavior is noted in the following example of extreme bravado, where aggressive behavior is desired and a clear distinction (based on bravery) between drive-by shootings and face-to-face shootings is clear. For example, Claude notes that, "if someone is getting shot in a drive-by and someone else gets hit, it is an accident. You know, I never do drive-bys. I walk up to them and shoot. I ain't trying to get anyone else shot to take care of business."

A final example of masculinity and bravado, as perceived by Mark, illustrates his commitment to being a stand-up guy, a person who will face the consequences of gang activity. The situation he discusses had to do with his current incarceration. Mark explains how he adhered to the gang value of not being a snitch by refusing to provide information about rival gang members' involvement in two homicides to the police, which could have helped in his prosecution for murder. He comments, "I know what I did [gang war murder]. You know what I mean? I'm not gonna take the easy way out [snitch on rival gangs for two homicides]. I know what I did. I'm facing my responsibility."

An interesting note in this scenario has to do with Mark's continued loyalty to the values of his gang when he was now in prison. His information on the rival gang's homicides most likely could have reduced the criminal charges against him and he subsequently would have received a lesser prison sentence. Taking into consideration that the inmate's cultural code is similar if not the same as the gang code, Mark was adhering to the same value system.

The image of toughness fits well under masculinity and bravado as an attribute positively perceived by the gang members who we interviewed. Its importance lies in projecting an image via reputation that conveys a definition of who the collective group is and what physical force they are willing to use when necessary. Charlie gives a clear explanation of this attribute in the statement that "everybody wants to fight for the power, for the next man to fear him. It's all about actually killing the motherfuckers and how many motherfuckers you can kill. Drive-by shootings is old school." The implication is that having a collective reputation for being powerful motivates Charlie. Charlie projects an image of toughness and power when he describes the image of shooting someone you are after and not hiding behind the random shooting characterized by drive-bys.

Other gang member interviewees prefer to define their toughness in terms of physical fighting without the use of any weapons, though it was often noted that it was too difficult to maintain a tough reputation under such conditions. For instance, the predicament in which Mark found himself was one where rival gangs used guns and other lethal instruments and, as a result of this, his reputation as an effective street fighter proved to be of little value. In short, his toughness and fighting skills were obsolete in life-threatening encounters.

MARK: Like my case, I'm a fighter. I don't like using guns. The only reason I bought a gun was because every time I got out of the car to fight, I'd have my ribs broken, the back of my head almost crushed with a baseball bat. I was tired of getting jumped. I couldn't get a fair fight. Nobody wanted to fight me because I had a bad reputation. Then, I decided, why even fight? Everybody else was pulling guns. It's either get out of the car and get killed or kill them.

The fact that Mark has good fighting skills ironically forced him to carry a gun. The rules of gang fighting found Mark outnumbered and unarmed, placing him in a vulnerable position. The proliferation of firearms among urban street gangs is well documented by Blumstein (1995b) and others. Lethal weapons, mainly firearms, drastically changed the defining characteristics of gang warfare in the late 1980s and 1990s, when most of the interviewed gang members were active in a gang in their community.

Reputation. On a collective group level, it was important to develop and maintain the gang's reputation of being a dangerous group to deal with, especially for other groups or individuals who posed a threat to their drug operations. Newton points out the necessity for communicating the gang's willingness to threaten the use of violence for retaliation against rivals. Guns often played an important role in the development and maintenance of reputation though, as Newton notes, they were rarely utilized in conflicting situations.

NEWTON: We had guns to fend off jackers, but we never had to use them, 'cause people knew we were straps. People knew our clique. They are not going to be stupid. We've gotten into a few arguments, but it never came to a gun battle. Even when we were gangbangin', we didn't use guns. We only fought off the Bloods.

Aside from a collective reputation, the group serves the identifying needs of its individual members (Kanter 1972). The gang members who we interviewed told us about their need to fall back on the reputation of their gang to help them develop their own reputation, which gave them a sense of fulfillment. In general, people want to present others with cues that will enhance desired typifications of who they are. They desire to present who they are in ways that will cause those with whom they interact to adhere to their situated claims (Hewitt and Stokes 1975). Wiley discusses the way that gang affiliation enhanced his reputation as a dangerous individual, a person not to be tested by others.

WILEY: There are people that know me. Even ones that are contemplating robbing me know of me from the gang experience. They know if you try and rob me [drugs and money], more than likely you gonna get killed. I was gonna protect what was mine. I'll die trying.

Sidney perceives gang membership differently. He attained a reputation through gang activity, and guns clearly played an important role in that process. He explains, "Fear and desire to have a reputation on the streets made me do it. When I got into the streets, I saw the glamour of it. I wanted a reputation there. What better way to get a reputation than to pick up a pistol. I've shot several people."

Although most gang members who we interviewed expressed a desire to be known in the community for some particular attribute, there were some who simply wanted to be known, sort of as in achieving celebrity status. Miquel notes, "You basically want people to know your name. It's kind of like politicians, like that, you wanna be known. In my generation you want somebody to say, 'I know him, he used to hang around with us.'"

Respect. Throughout the interviews of gang members, the subject of disrespect was associated in gang vernacular with retaliatory violence. Interactions with rivals stemming from an affront to a gang member's self-image often became the excuse to use a gun to redeem his or her reputational identity. Strauss (1969) argues that anger and withdrawal occur when a person is confronted with a possible loss of face. For the gang members in this study, such anger was apparent when rivals challenged their self-identity (i.e., when they were disrespected).

According to these gang members, disrespect, or rejection of self-professed identity claims by others, often was the cause of violence. Violence was even more likely to be the result of disrespect when no retaliatory action could lead to a loss of face. Wiley relates his view on this subject in general terms, "Violence starts to escalate once you start to disrespect me. Once you start to second-guess my manhood, I'll fuck you up. You start coming at me with threats, then I feel offended. Once I feel offended, I react violently. That's how I was taught to react." The idea of his manhood being threatened seems to be directly associated with Strauss's (1962) concept of identity denial by an accusing other. This threat to a gang member's masculinity by not recognizing another's status claims is apparently an extremely serious breach of gang etiquette. Claude explains this attitude.

CLAUDE: When someone disrespects me, they are putting my manhood in jeopardy. They are saying my words are shit, or putting my family in danger. . . . Most of the time I do it [use violence] to make people feel the pain or hurt that I feel. I don't know no other way to do it, as far as expressing myself any other way.

Hickman and Kuhn (1956) point out that the self anchors people in every situation in which they are involved. These authors claim that, unlike other objects, the self is present in all interactions and serves as the basis from which we all make judgments and plans of reaction toward others that are part of a given situation. When being confronted by gang rivals who have been perceived as insulting an opposing gang member, the definition of street norms calls for an exaggerated response. That is, the disrespectful words must be countered with serious physical force to justify the disrespected individual's maintenance of self (or manhood). A prime example of feeling disrespected is discussed in terms of territory and the unwritten rules of the street by Mark, a gang member who told us about an encounter with a rival gang that disrespected him to the point that he was left with no other alternative choice of action but to shoot them. He explains, "So, as we were fighting, they started saying that this was their neighborhood and started throwing their gang signs. To me, to let somebody do that to me is disrespect. So I told them where I was from." A little while later, the gang members in question showed up in Mark's neighborhood and shot at him as he was walking with his two small children to a convenience store to get ice cream. Mark continues to recite the tale.

MARK: I was just so mad and angry for somebody to disrespect me like that and shoot. We got a rule on the street. There is rules. You don't shoot at anybody if there is kids. That's one of the main rules of the street. They broke the rules. To me, that was telling me that they didn't have no respect for me or my kids. So that's how I lost it and shot them. I was so disrespected that I didn't know how to handle it.

The notion of disrespect is analogous to an attack on the self. Because many of the gang members in our sample reported that masculinity is an important attribute of self, they believed any disrespect was a direct threat to their masculinity. For those brought up in impoverished, high-crime communities, as these study participants were, there are limited alternatives to such conflicting situations (Anderson 1999). Retaliation to redeem one's self-identity in terms of their internalized concept of manhood precludes a violent reaction to all actions of insult. To gang members caught in those confrontational encounters, there is a very limited course of action: that of perpetrating violence toward those who threaten their self-concept of who they perceive themselves to be.

Gangs and Guns

The perceived necessity by gang members to carry handguns became a reality for the participants in this study. They collectively expressed the dangerousness of their life on the street, whether it was selling narcotics, committing a robbery, being a provocateur against rivals, or being the recipient of violent retaliation on the part of perceived enemies. These gang members viewed their world fraught with potential danger; thus, the need for the possession of guns. It is necessary, then, to take the person's definitions of the situation into account in explaining their unlawful conduct (Hewitt 1988). Often the interviewees emphasized the importance of the gun as an attribute that communicated their masculinity in some situations, but was also seen as protection in others. Quite often both definitions of the situation existed simultaneously.

The analysis of the interview data dichotomized those gun-using encounters as either expressions of power or protection based on each gang member's perceived definition of the situation. Carrying a firearm elicits various feelings of power. Claude notes that, "when I have a gun, I feel like I'm on top of it, like I'm superman or something. You got to let them know." Miquel explains that the larger the gun the more powerful he felt, "I was 15 at that point in time and I had a fascination with guns. It was like the more powerful impact the gun had, the more fascinated I got and the more I wanted it."

The actual use of a firearm is described in a situation that most lethally expressed the power of guns in an attempt to injure those belonging to rival gangs. In this situation, Wiley points out that they were not trying to injure or kill anyone for personal reasons, but rather to display a sense of willingness to commit a lethal act for purposes of dominance.

WILEY: When I was younger, we used to do drive-bys. It didn't matter who you were. We didn't go after a specific person. We went after a specific group. Whoever is standing at a particular house or wherever you may be, and you're grouped up and have the wrong color on just because you were in a rival gang. You didn't have to do anything to us to come get you, it was a spontaneous reaction.

When not being involved in collective gang violence, individual members found themselves being involved in gun use situations as instigators when confronting rivals on their own. Trent remarks, "My cousin told me if you pull it, you better use it. So you gotta boost yourself. When the time came, I was just shooting."

This study found that the majority of these violent gun-using situations involved individuals as opposed to large numbers of gang members confronting each other with firearms. Yet we were told by the interviewees that, in gang representation either on an individual basis or in a small group, whether it be in a protective or retaliatory mode, gang members had to display a power position to those confronting them to maintain their reputations. They emphasized that guns were important in that respect.

The issues surrounding gun possession often have to do with interpersonal conflict as opposed to collective gang situations. The fear of being physically harmed within their residential environment, coupled with the relative ease in which a person can attain a firearm, has resulted in a proliferation of weapons in the community. Growing up in such high-crime neighborhoods and then joining a gang can shape a minority teen's perceptions of his or her social world. Giselle explains, "There's a lot of brutality. There is a lot of murder around us. There is a lot of violence—period. There are enemies and all. A lot of pressure, you know. If you're not going to do this, then they're going to do it to you. I'd rather get caught with a gun than without." The perceived fear for potential harm caused Giselle to carry a gun when outside of her home. As she expresses the violence that is prevalent in her environment, she is also relating how random threats can often occur and that she sees the necessity to harm rivals before they harm her.

According to Orval, individually or collectively, rival gang members constantly pose a physical threat. He also discusses the need for protection and how drug sales caused him to be a target for those who would try and rob him.

ORVAL: Carried a gun because I knew what I was doing, especially since I was in a gang. Other gangs are gonna try and come after us. So I used it [gun] against those gangs and to make sure that my investments in the drugs was protected. I don't want nobody to take money from me.

Lastly, Wiley relates the need to carry a gun at all times to protect his jewelry, which he openly displays as a symbol of his monetary success through the use of illegal means.

WILEY: I basically carried a gun for protection, just like you have a best friend. You and your best friend go everywhere. I got over $10,000 of jewelry on me. People see all this jewelry and may try and beat me up. There may be two or three and just myself.

All of the descriptive attributes related by the gang members in the study population played an important role in shaping their individual gang identity. The roles they learned to play through their processional development into bona fide gang members were accomplished by group socialization. Acting on those perceived valued attributes resulted in their transformed identity. Once the socialization process is complete, the novice gang member has to sustain his or her reputation and status personally as well as collectively with the formal group.

> An individual who implicitly or explicitly signifies that he has certain social characteristics ought in fact to be what he claims he is. In consequence, when an individual projects a definition of the situation and thereby makes an implicit or explicit claim to be a person of a particular kind, he automatically exerts a moral demand upon others, obliging them to value and treat him in the manner that persons of his kind have a right to expect. (Goffman 1959:4)

Based on Goffman's findings, the sense of self of the gang members in this study was directly affected by the claims (attributes) that they desired to convey to others about who they perceived themselves to be.

Discussion

Gangs not only fulfill specific needs for individuals that other groups in disadvantaged neighborhoods may fail to provide but, as our interviews suggest, they also are important primary groups into which individuals become socialized. It thus is not surprising that self-con-

71

cept and identity are closely tied to gang membership. Guns are also important in this regard. We propose that, for the gang members in this sample, gang-related gun violence can be understood in terms of self and identity that are created through the process of socialization and are heavily rooted in notions of masculinity. Therefore, this analysis provides insight into the way gang socialization can produce violence, especially gun-related violence.

Parallel to the issue of gun violence, we find that the possession and use of guns among gang members is important because, in addition to protecting gang members, guns are tools that aid in identity formation and impression management. As many of the narratives suggest, guns were often connected in some way to masculine attributes. Gang members told us that they often used guns to project their reputation or reclaim respect. We believe that the consequences of these findings regarding gang violence and guns are important for public policy for three reasons.

First, because this sample consisted only of gang members who had committed the most severe forms of violence (i.e., they were incarcerated for relatively long periods of time for their gun-related violence), there may be some interest in targeting similar individuals early in their criminal careers to "diminish the pool of chronic gang offenders" (Piehl, Kennedy, and Braga 2000:100). We believe this may be one potential method for reducing gang-related violence because the gang members in this study often had extensive violent histories. Moreover, in other studies of gang violence, researchers have generally found that a small number of offenders commit most of the crimes. For instance, Kennedy, Piehl, and Braga (1996) find that less than 1 percent of Boston's youth were responsible for nearly 60 percent of the city's homicides. Thus, identifying the rather small pool of chronic gang members may be a useful approach to reducing gang violence because they are the ones engaged in most of the violence. This approach, however, is somewhat problematic because identifying chronic offenders is both difficult and controversial (Walker 1998). Moreover, Spergel and Curry (1990), who studied the effectiveness of various gang-related intervention strategies, argue that law enforcement efforts seem to be one of the least effective methods for reducing gang-related problems.

Second, this research suggests that policies aimed at reducing gang violence should take gang socialization into account. Simply reducing gun availability through law enforcement crackdowns on violent gang members is probably not sufficient (see Piehl, Kennedy, and Braga 2000). In addition, the interviews with these gang members suggest that guns probably are far more important to the daily lives and identities of gang members than most policymakers might imagine, precisely because they help project a reputation and create respect. Thus, if gang culture could be changed through the resocialization of gang members, gun-related gang violence might decrease significantly. Indeed, studies of gun initiatives, such as the Boston Gun Project, suggest that gang violence is reduced when gang culture is changed. As Piehl, Kennedy, and Braga point out, one reason that homicides decreased as a result of the Boston Gun Project was because that initiative focused on "establishing and/or reinforcing nonviolent norms by increasing peer support for eschewing violence, by improving young people's handling of potentially violent situations" (2000:100).

Overall, however, the strategy of focusing on gang socialization falls most closely in line with social intervention perspectives that have not proved to be highly successful in various situations (Shelden, Tracy, and Brown 2001). Therefore, altering the values of gang members to reduce the likelihood of gang-related violence might not be the most promising approach to reducing gang violence. As Klein suggests, "[g]angs are by-products of their communities: They cannot long be controlled by attacks on symptoms alone; the community structure and capacity must also be targeted" (1995:147). Whether gang violence can be reduced by the resocialization of gang members appears to remain open to debate, but it clearly is one avenue of intervention that requires further attention in the research.

Third, it is not clear from this research whether simply eliminating or reducing access to guns can reduce gun-related gang violence. For example, studies like the Youth Firearms Violence Initiative conducted by the Justice Department's Office of Community Oriented Policing Services suggest that gun violence can be reduced by focusing, at least in part, on reducing access to guns (Dunworth 2000). However, that study also indicates that, once the projects focusing on access to guns end, gang violence increases to previous levels. Moreover, the interviews that we conducted with gang members suggest there is little reason to believe that they would be any less likely to look to gangs as a source of status and protection and may use other weapons, though arguably less lethal than guns, to aid in transformations of identity and preserve a sense of self. Thus, although reduction strategies (see also Braga et al. 2008) may prevent gang-related violence in the short term, there is little evidence that this intervention strategy will have long-term effects because it does not adequately deal with gang culture and processes of gang socialization.

On the whole, the findings of this study suggest that gang socialization produces gang-related gun violence through changes to identify and self. Although the problems of gang-related violence appear to play out at the micro level, the solutions to these problems do not appear to be overwhelmingly situated at this level. Instead, we believe that intervention efforts must reside at the macro level and impact socialization processes at the micro level. We agree with Short that "absent change in macro level forces associated with [gang violence], vulnerable individuals will continue to be produced" (1997:181; see also Shelden, Tracy, and Brown 2001). Thus, it may be more fruitful to focus on societal intervention efforts aimed at improving the economic and social environments that create gangs. Having identified gangs as important sources of socialization for members into lives that involve guns and violent crime, we turn our attention to a related question: Now that these individuals are out of the gang environment or other previous social locations and in prison, what changes occur in their views of guns?

4

How Incarceration Shapes Views and the Use of Guns

PROTECTION IS ONE OF THE MOST COMMON REASONS PEOPLE give for owning a gun (Cooke 2004; Lizotte and Bordua 1980; Shapiro et al 1997; Sheley and Wright 1995; Wright and Rossi 1986; Wright, Rossi, and Daly 1983). This is true of criminals as well as the general public. In this chapter, we explore the transformation experienced by the inmates who we interviewed regarding perceptions of gun use as a result of their prison socialization. Wright and Rossi find that, "among incarcerated gun criminals, self protection was the single most important motive" for obtaining their most recent handgun (1986:139). Although protection is the central reason that many inmates said that they would possess and carry a handgun, power is also an important motivator. We were surprised to discover how many interviewees commented on the importance of guns in projecting an image of power (Diener and Kerber 1979). We also examine the concepts of power and protection and the importance of these concepts to inmates' beliefs about why others carry guns. We found that their beliefs about guns changed according to the amount of time they had spent in prison. The longer inmates were incarcerated, the more likely they were to believe that people carry guns to project power. We believe that prison socialization helps to explain these observations and argue that changing attitudes toward guns in prison could be counterproductive and make inmates more likely to carry guns once they are released from prison.

Prison Socialization

Prisons are often described as micro "functioning societies" (Sykes 1974) or "total institutions" (Goffman 1961b), which have a structure and culture that exercise a great deal of influence over inmates' lives. Drawing from the idea that prison is like a microsociety, Clemmer developed the term "prisonization" to describe the process of being socialized into prison life. According to Clemmer, *prisonization* can be defined as the acceptance of "folkways, mores, customs, and general culture of the penitentiary" (1940:270). Over time, the inmates in this study became immersed in prison culture.

Although prisonization has been studied extensively (see Atchley and McCabe 1968; Gillespie 2003; Wheeler 1961) and the idea is relatively straightforward, the cause of the prison culture that does the socializing is more obscure. Specifically, sociologists have argued that prisonization is the result of deprivation, importation, or both (Dhami, Ayton, and Loewenstein 2007). According to the deprivation model, prisonization is a way of coping with the "pains of imprisonment" (Sykes 1974; see also Gendreau and Keyes 2001; Kalnich and Stojkovic 1985). Some of the inmates we talked with clearly told us that prison life was stressful and had changed the way they viewed the world. For example, Wiley, a 21-year-old serving 25 years for aggravated assault with a gun, explains how he changed.

WILEY: I don't normally go to the yard, the gym, and it's not because I am afraid of anybody. I go out there as a man and deal with whatever comes to me as a man. Secondly, I got one of the coldest crews in this prison. You know, we are together, we'll sow a motherfucker up. But because I got objectives and goals to get out of here, kids to feed, and this, that, and the other, I now choose not to go out to the yard and gym as much because I am tired of seeing the fights. I've seen almost a thousand fights in here and they're all the same. It's boring now to see someone get beat up. . . . In some instances, I feel so bad that it makes me want to go to clunk the guy—give him a taste of his own medicine.

Wiley claims to have changed in prison, but many of the other inmates we interviewed explain that people come to prison ready to exploit other inmates. The suggestion that inmates come to prison and shape prison culture is synonymous with the importation model that proposes prisonization is the result of ideas, attitudes, and behaviors that inmates bring into prison from the outside (Irwin and Cressey 1962). Eloy, another 21-year-old convicted of first-degree murder, explains this.

> Eloy: I got committed.
>
> Interviewer: But this was your first violation with guns? Tell me a little more about this.
>
> Eloy: My homeboy, I was already bad before I got caught. I was already a gang member.

We argue that both importation and deprivation are important, and they create a unique cultural milieu that influences the beliefs of inmates and their behaviors while in prison (see also Jiang and Fisher-Giorlando 2002). This cultural milieu associated with prison life then intensifies the inmates' beliefs and values about guns and gun violence. We noticed this specifically in the case of power.

Power and Prison Culture

One aspect of prison life that has been written about in the prison literature is power. Weber (1969) points out that power is simply the probability that orders and regulations will be obeyed. Sykes suggested that prisons are "organized around a grant of power which is without an equal in American society" (1974:42). We often encountered this concept of power in inmate narratives about simple day-to-day interactions. Sometimes notions about power were stated directly. As Edwin put it, "My behavior in here [prison] reflects the need for power and control . . . to control the situation and to have it go my way." At other times, the notion of power was present just below the surface of an inmate's narrative. For example, Chance employs notions of needing power in prison to survive.

> Chance: Yeah, I mean, you know a dude threaten you—to do something to you. Man, up in here you got to be . . . you got . . . you know, come out of here whole, you know? Livin'.
>
> Interviewer: Right.
>
> Chance: So, you know, you try to take the things that people say up in here a little more seriously than you do people out there.
>
> Interviewer: Right.

CHANCE: You know what I mean? You can walk away from something out there but, in here, you're around these cats everyday and you cannot walk away. So what you got to do is hammer it or leave it alone.

Another interviewee, Beau, claims that inmates must assert their power when they enter the prison or they will be taken advantage of throughout the time they are incarcerated.

BEAU: If you can't earn your respect one way, you're going to earn it another. Whether I beat your ass or you beat mine, either one, it don't matter, you're going to get your respect and that's what kids are learning today.

INTERVIEWER: Look at you here, let's be honest, you're in here and respect's a big deal for you in here now.

BEAU: Yes, it has to be.

INTERVIEWER: You can't just be an average inmate.

BEAU: You can't show weakness.

INTERVIEWER: Yeah, I understand that. But the other guys don't know how to dance and do okay. Not everybody belongs to a gang.

BEAU: They're called punks, bitches, whatever. . . . You're going to have to show something sooner or later or someone's going to hurt you. Basically, you judge people by heart, how much heart they have. And even if you show a little bit of heart, they'll still respect you, 'cause you're trying. It's the people that don't show any.

Prison staff also project images of power from the moment an inmate enters the prison. For instance, Goffman's influential work on asylums, which has often been extended to prisons, notes that, when a new inmate enters the institution, "the initial moments of socialization may involve an obedience test and even a will-breaking contest: an inmate who shows defiance receives immediate visible punishment, which increases until he openly cries uncle and humbles himself" (1961b:17).

For many of the inmates who we interviewed, the reality of prison life means that state power is defective to the extent that there are not enough prison staff to monitor each prisoner. As both Edwin and Chance suggest, inmates have little security and must rely on themselves or other inmates for protection. Thus, power is transferred from the custodians to the inmates. This transfer of power

makes power central to inmates' lives. We believe that the prisonization process means that nearly all inmates will eventually come to
strongly view guns as symbols of power. In his research, Sykes discovered that inmates describe power within prison in relationship to
access to implements of power, including guns. As one inmate who
Sykes interviewed put it, "[t]hey have the guns and we don't"
(1974:41).

Themes in Prison Culture

Researchers studying aspects of prisonization pay particular attention
to the "prison code" (Ross and Richards 2003). The prison code is a
set of rules that inmates live by. These rules are essentially the most
important norms of prison culture. At the top of the prison hierarchy
are those inmates that excel at the norms of prison life (Irwin 1970).
Part of the prison code includes projecting an image of fearlessness
and power (Tromanhauser 2003; Walters 2003). Inmates who back
down from confrontations are viewed as weak and are often looked
on negatively by other inmates. It is within this cultural milieu that
inmates' attitudes toward powerful inmates are generally positive
while attitudes toward victims are generally negative (Ireland 2002).
As Chance explained earlier, even inmates who try to keep clear of
violence are aware that they must project an image of power to do so.
Moreover, studies on prison culture suggest that prison violence is
often an expression of power carried out by those inmates at the top
of the prison hierarchy (Knowles 1999; Tucker 1982). Our interviews
of inmates led us to believe that prison culture should shape the "personality of the ruled," especially with respect to their attitudes toward
gun possession (Sykes 1974:xvi). These changing attitudes may
shape inmates' willingness to carry guns in the future.

Prison culture and attitudes toward carrying guns. Within the
prison culture, specific perceptions about why people carry guns
should change over time as attitudes and values change in response to
prison conditions. For newly arrived inmates, prison is often a place
of insecurity. Indeed, prison research has suggested that inmate violence is most likely to occur during the early phases of prison sentences (Bottoms 1999; Harer and Langan 2001; Memory et al. 1999).
Harer and Langan (2001), for instance, argue that higher levels of
instrumental violence occur when inmates are initially incarcerated.

Inmates we talked with were likely to use violence to protect themselves and show that they will not become victims. It was not uncommon for us to talk with inmates who had recently been incarcerated and then placed on administrative segregation for fighting. For instance, one interviewer's notes read as follows.

> This is an interview on inmate Ricardo [age 21 who was just two years into his life sentence for murder]. We weren't able to tape-record this interview because Mr. Ricardo was in administrative segregation due to some difficulties he had had with another inmate. Apparently, Ricardo was fighting. The interview was done through the phone system because of his administrative segregation status, and therefore what I did was took notes and, from those notes, I'll just dictate the responses to the research questions.

Jones and Schmid (2000:54) have pointed out that novice inmates are often overwhelmed by their sense of fear and therefore are primarily concerned with protection. Moreover, these inmates tend to view prison as "violent and uncertain." Based on the prisonization literature, it is hypothesized that relatively novice inmate accounts of perceptions about gun carrying should be influenced by their lack of prisonization. Thus, their gun accounts should focus mainly on self-defense. New inmates are likely to project their insecurity and need for protection onto others and should emphasize that others carry guns for instrumental reasons like protection.

We believe that, in the case of the inmates who we interviewed, the early years in prison were fundamentally different than later years (see also Gillespie 2003). As these inmates came to understand prison culture, their initial feelings of uncertainty diminished and they did not worry as much as new inmates about how to secure their safety. That is, many "inmates" are transformed into "convicts" (Blomberg and Lucken 2000).

Novice inmates who were not socialized into prison life often expressed concern during the interviews about the prison social organization and implementing the norms of prison life to avoid violence. More experienced inmates told us that they had learned to survive. Antwan (incarcerated for nearly five years) remarks, "I don't know. I guess in here you learn a lot of different things. It's a dangerous atmosphere in here. So I mean you learn, just learn to survive in here." McCorkle (1992:161) argues that, throughout the duration of imprisonment, an inmate gains an understanding of how to avoid being subjugated by projecting an image of violence and power to others. As a result, many inmates find ways to carry weapons. Research shows that inmates often use violence and threats as a "form of pre-emptive self defense" (McCorkle 1992:161).

We argue that, as feelings of uncertainty about prison life decrease, power becomes more central to inmates. For instance, research has documented that there is a strong positive relationship between bullying and social status (Ireland 2002). Thus, prison life becomes organized around obtaining power for status. Power, consequently, should be more central to an inmate's sense of self among more experienced inmates. For experienced inmates, violence is more likely to be an expressive show of power over weaker inmates. The more experienced inmates who we interviewed understood that social status is tied to projections of power within the institution. Thus, these inmates were primarily concerned with status and power as opposed to protection. Experienced inmates often projected their desire for power on others and their accounts of why people carry guns tended to emphasize the expressive reason "to feel powerful." The remainder of this chapter focuses on what the inmates say about the reasons that people carry guns and how that is related to their prisonization experiences. Prior to examining these inmate accounts, however, we discuss the methods that we used for coding the qualitative data.

To display the trends that we observed in our qualitative data, each interview was coded to determine whether inmates gave accounts of guns as objects of power, protection, or both. When the inmates did not use the words "power" or "protection" to describe the reasons that others carry a gun, their responses were coded based on statements that appeared to best describe those concepts. For instance, statements like "people carry guns to feel secure" were coded as consistent with themes of protection and statements like "people carry guns because they can use them to influence others" were coded as consistent with themes of power. In most cases, however, such coding was not necessary because inmates used the words "power" or "protection" to describe people's motivations for possessing guns. It is important to point out that inmates did mention that people have guns for reasons other than power or protection. For instance, 17 inmates reported that people carry guns for "criminal activity." In addition, some inmates said that people carry guns for hunting. Finally, a few inmates said that other people carry guns because "you never know what will happen." Even though we often prompted the interviewees to elaborate on such vague accounts, it still was not possible to code these responses as consistent with concepts of power or protection.

Figure 4.1 sums up the qualitative findings empirically. It shows the results of that coding according to the number of years that inmates had been incarcerated. The three time periods (three years or less, three years to eight years, and more than eight years) were chosen because they most accurately display the trends that emerged from the interviews of inmates. That is, these three time periods provided natural breaks in the data with respect to the distribution of power and protection. Of the inmates interviewed who spent three years or less in prison during their current sentence of incarceration ($n = 16$), 56 percent ($n = 9$) said that other people are motivated to carry guns for protection while 25 percent ($n = 4$) of those inmates said that people carry guns because they are motivated by power. The remaining inmates said that they carry guns for

Figure 4.1 Inmate Accounts of Why Others Carry Guns, by Length of Incarceration ($n = 61$)

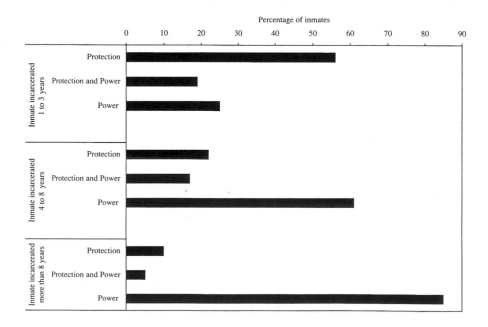

both protection and power ($n = 3$). For the inmates incarcerated over eight years, however, 10 percent ($n = 2$) said that protection is one of the main motivations that people carry guns and 85 percent ($n = 17$) said that power is one of the main reasons that people carry guns. The 23 inmates incarcerated for more than three years but less than eight years were more mixed in their responses with 22 percent ($n = 5$) saying that people carry guns for protection and 61 percent ($n = 14$) saying that people carry guns for power. Approximately 17 percent ($n = 4$) said that people carry guns for protection and power. It therefore appears that inmates' perceptions about why people possess guns are mainly focused on protection among newly incarcerated inmates and on power among experienced inmates. These results confirm what was observed in the qualitative data. Overall, Figure 4.1 clearly denotes the trend in accounts of power and protection by the inmates in this sample. Over time, inmates are likely to say that the reason people carry guns is to feel powerful. It is important to remember that all of these inmates were sentenced for using a gun in the commission of a violent crime and that these results do not appear to be related to the type of crime that an inmate committed.

Guns as Protection

Novice inmates who we talked with were more likely to perceive that others needed guns for protection. Claude, a young gang member convicted of attempted murder for shooting an acquaintance who disrespected him, had been incarcerated for approximately two years and had spent most of that time in administrative segregation for fighting with other inmates. Consistent with importation models of prisonization, Claude talks a great deal about the importance of respect, retaliation, and power while on the "outside." Claude believes that guns prevented people from doing harm to one another. When Claude is questioned directly about his perception about the reasons that other people carry guns, however, he speaks mostly about the importance of protection.

INTERVIEWER: Why do you think people carry guns?
CLAUDE: Protection you know. Other people carry guns, you know what I'm saying, because they are protected by them. Most gang

members carry them for protection, or they want to be hard ass. So that's how that is.

It is interesting to note that Claude's account of guns as protection does not differ significantly from the female gang members who we interviewed. For instance, Giselle, a recently incarcerated 20-year-old female inmate, feels that possessing a gun made most people feel safe.

INTERVIEWER: Why do you think most people carry guns?
GISELLE: For protection. To feel safe. No one can depend on the enforcement as much maybe as 30 to 40 years ago.

Giselle's experiences are likely shaped by her degree of socialization in the prison culture. Like Claude, Giselle refers to reputation, disrespect, and power while talking about life on the outside. Unlike Claude, however, Giselle is not afraid to admit that prison frightens her.

INTERVIEWER: Being here, what kind of an effect has that had on you?
GISELLE: I have gotten so fragile, scared almost of everything. I mean I won't even carry things in a certain way if I know I have a chance of hurting somebody. I walk on the sidewalk way away from the little bunnies and the frogs. I'm scared to step on them.

Although nearly all newly incarcerated inmates argued that other people's motivations for possessing guns are largely for protection, a few also answered in reference to their own experiences. Rodney, who admitted to several armed robberies and had been incarcerated three years, appeared to be less socialized to the prison environment than many other inmates in the sample. Rodney admits that he is not adjusting well to prison life. Unlike many of his peers who had been incarcerated for some time, Rodney keeps in frequent contact with his family because they are "all I got right now since I'm locked up." Rodney argues that guns simply provide him with a sense of protection.

INTERVIEWER: Why do you think people carry guns?
RODNEY: For me, I think people feel a sense of security. For example, you're at a party and there's those certain people at the party. You have a pistol. You figure I show up and anybody tries to start anything or anything happens, all you got to do is pull it out. . . . A sense

of security, that's what it was to me. I felt real secure like I wasn't going to be messed.

A more extreme example is Johnathan, a new inmate who had been sentenced (a second time) for assault. Johnathan notes that he is currently working in the prison therapeutic community to change himself and others. He feels that everyone should be "more empathetic." Johnathan willingly tells us that he has no "write-ups" and obeys prison rules so that he can "get paroled." These statements appear to be more consistent with prisonized inmates. When Johnathan talks about possessing a gun prior to prison life, however, he says it was largely for reasons related to power. He argues that he would now like a gun for protection from other inmates who might do him harm. He persists in this account despite the fact that inmates obviously are not allowed to possess a gun in prison.

INTERVIEWER: Why do you think people carry guns?
JOHNATHAN: When I was younger, when I used a gun it was a tool to take and scare people. Now, it's become a tool like a pacifier almost, without your weapon you feel insecure 'cause you have no security in here.

Thus, for Johnathan, it appears that the reasons other people carry a guns is a reflection of his own feelings of needing to be secure. He argues that a gun would provide him with a sense of security by deterring others from exploiting or assaulting him.

Inmates who are incarcerated for gun-related armed robberies give similar accounts of why people possess guns. Although armed robbers are more likely to view guns as tools of the trade (e.g., objects of power that get victims to comply with orders), they appear to be no different than other recently incarcerated inmates in their accounts of why people carry guns. For instance, Isaiah, who had been incarcerated for only a few years and often mentions that he wants to be in control of situations and people, argues that "handguns are for one purpose . . . personal protection."

Guns as Protection and Symbols of Power

The interviews with inmates also suggest that some of them are likely to refer to people's motivations to carry guns in terms of both protection and power. In a few instances, it was difficult to distinguish which account—protection or power—was more central to the answers given by the interviewees. Matthew, a 42-year-old who had been incarcerated for four years for second-degree murder, believes that people carry guns for "protection and power." He argues that, to determine the motives people have for possessing a gun, it often is possible to look at the caliber of the gun they are carrying. Large guns are possessed for power and small guns for protection.

INTERVIEWER: Why do people carry guns?
MATTHEW: [People] carry them for protection and for power. When I say that, what I'm talking about is people who are scary out there and you got people that just don't care about nobody. They're nothing without it. People who need that, who didn't get what they were suppose to get at home. Now, they get a gun and now they're somebody. People are just scared, that's why they carry it.
INTERVIEWER: What types of guns do they carry?
MATTHEW: Small handguns—.20s, .25s, and .30s. Some even carry .44s and 9 millimeters. But mainly I could say that the people that I've known that carry guns for protection carry small handguns. They don't want a big gun. They just want something to warn somebody off in case something happens.
INTERVIEWER: What about criminals, do they carry bigger guns?
MATTHEW: Yes. They want bigger guns. They want to feel that power. They want to show. That's what it's all about—the show.

Matthew is typical of inmates incarcerated for about four years who begin suggesting that power is an important motivator for gun possession. Thus, although inmates' accounts of protection are still important, power also appears to figure quite prominently in accounts given by offenders incarcerated over three but under six years. Compared to inmates incarcerated under three years (such as Claude), the focus on power is much more prominent in these accounts.

Stephen, with no previous criminal history, had been incarcerated for nearly four years for murdering his business partner. Stephen clearly imports more conventional norms into prison and therefore is struggling to survive and make sense of his surroundings. He repeatedly refers to people on the inside as having a "lack of respect," but also sets himself apart from other inmates who have committed similar crimes as though he is somehow different. He admits that he is having a difficult time surviving in prison, but also notes, like other inmates who have been locked up for approximately the same amount of time, that many people carry guns for power and protection.

INTERVIEWER: Why do people carry guns?
STEPHEN: Some people are scared. I think some people are thinking the power. They have a gun, they have the power. These people [other inmates] doesn't have no education at all for guns. None whatsoever. You know, I overhear . . . I hear the kids, especially kids . . . sometime I cry. God knows I cry.

Kent is one of the few recently incarcerated inmates who does not say that protection is an important reason that others carry guns. Unlike most of these inmates, however, Kent had previously been incarcerated for several years in an adult facility. At the time of the interview, Kent had been incarcerated for less than one year for first-degree murder.

INTERVIEWER: Why do people carry guns?
KENT: The guys that I know in Denver I'd say because, when you have that gun, it gives like, uh, a sense of, uh, like you have all the power. You just feel untouchable. I mean . . . that's the feeling I got off them guys when they carried guns.

It may be that Kent's prior prison experiences socialized him to the prison culture and he was able to adjust to the uncertainties of prison life much more quickly than most first timers. Although Kent initially says that he is just doing his time and "try[ing] not to talk to people in here," he also goes on to reveal that he is working to change new inmates' views of the world.

KENT: I try to talk to them and tell them, "Look, you know, you guys, you gotta find another way because I mean, yeah, you might think you're all cool in here acting the way you act. But what if your mom was in here to see how you were acting and you'd feel ashamed of yourself?" You know, I just try to give guys little . . . little seeds in their minds so they think, you know, maybe something will help them think different.

Thus, Kent's statement about socializing other inmates about their unacceptable behavior by referencing the outside world (their mother) is not typical of the other inmates who generally indicate that they "stay out of other people's business." However, like many of the more experienced inmates, Kent does talk about his efforts to inform younger inmates how to behave on the inside.

Guns as Symbols of Power

We found that, after longer periods of incarceration, most inmates stopped insisting that others carry guns for protection and instead said that others carry guns to "feel powerful." Indeed, only two inmates who were incarcerated eight years or longer argued that people carry guns for protection. Inmates incarcerated for longer periods of time instead focused on people's motives for carrying guns in terms of power. These accounts stand in sharp contrast to those of inmates who were incarcerated for shorter periods of time. Darrel, who had been incarcerated for nearly 10 years, probably sums up the position of the most experienced inmates best, "The way the bullets are made and the amount of powder they put in them, the way the guns are set up, they are only good for one thing—to knock down power on a person."

Edwin, who had been incarcerated for nine years for murder, appears to have adjusted well to prison life. He remarks that he is doing easy time, "You have a 13-inch color TV, ice cream on Sundays, air conditioning in our rooms, clean sheets delivered one day a week . . . and they call this prison!" Like other inmates in his position, Edwin believes that the only reason that people carry guns is because they seek power.

> INTERVIEWER: Why do you think people carry guns?
> EDWIN: A gun can be a tool of power, without a doubt. I think, it's just my opinion, but that's where the problem comes in. Powerless people, powerless-feeling people, are the people that commit crimes with handguns. Again, my only frame of reference is myself—it gave me a sense of power.
> INTERVIEWER: Right, right. . . .
> EDWIN: I had a collection of guns—several pistols, several rifles. And the most common caliber of handgun that I had was, Guess

what? .44 Magnum—Dirty Harry. I can be cool. Look at this, I can shoot the most powerful handgun in the world. I'm bad!

Again, references to power extend beyond the inmates' simple accounts about why other people carry guns. Several inmates projected their own experiences to others' motivations for carrying a gun. Ernesto provides an example of this type of self-projection. Ernesto, who had been convicted of robbery and incarcerated for nearly nine years, put it this way.

INTERVIEWER: Why do you think people carry guns?
ERNESTO: Ah, as far as I think, I think, I think weapons takes people from faith and gives them a sense of power.
INTERVIEWER: Uh-huh.
ERNESTO: And by using that weapon, they are expecting their sense of power that they have over another person. Knowing that you control that person's life 'cause you carry a weapon, and you know on any given time you can take that person's life from them. So the reason why people probably would carry guns in my environment, where I grew up, is having that . . . that sense of power. . . . So that feeling of being almost like God.
INTERVIEWER: Uh, so you think that it's power? And and, when, when would you come to use that power?
ERNESTO: Well, I mean, any I know, I've been around people that carry guns that, that have, that have initiated arguments just so they can show somebody that they have a gun, like "Hey dog, like mind, mind what you say, you know, I could take your life at any moment." That's everybody. That's every person. Everybody likes to be in power.

Russ, who appears concerned about the violent young offenders he observes coming into prison, has been incarcerated nearly eight years for murder. Like Kent, Russ says that he tried to help new inmates understand the norms of prison life, "You've got a lot of these young gangbangers coming in [to prison]. I try to talk to 'em. They're just so . . . they're . . . they're so set in their ways, you know? Like, I mean, I look at them and say, 'Oh, I was like that,' you know? You couldn't tell me nothin'. There was no reasoning." Russ also believes that power is the main reason that most people carry guns, "Most people, I believe, carry guns for the power it gives 'em. It gives me a superior power over you. . . . I mean, you might be, you might be much more bigger and stronger than me, but the moment I pull that gun out, that changes it. And if I know you got a gun, I'm damn sure I'm gonna have mine."

Jerry, who had been incarcerated nearly seven years, views guns mainly from his experiences as an armed robber. He also argues that guns give him a sense of power. He feels that others carry guns because they feel powerful. Moreover, unlike some inmates who feel that people carry guns for other reasons in addition to power (such as criminal activity, protection, hunting, or simply because they never know what might happen), Jerry points out that power is the only reason that people carry guns.

INTERVIEWER: When . . . why do you think people carry guns?

JERRY: Um, a gun is certainly most, uh, a symbol of authority, you know what I mean? If you have it, people are gonna say, "Hey, he has, you know, the power. He has the power in the situation right now, so I'm gonna pretty much give him everything that he wants," you know?

INTERVIEWER: An intimidation kind of thing?

JERRY: Yeah. So, you know and, when a person sees that, you know, they're like, "Hey, I'm . . . I'm on a power." Uh . . . uh . . . uh . . . hunger, you know? I . . . I want that power all the time so I'm gonna carry this gun, you know? And I'm gonna use the gun in this crime because I know people are gonna respect me more and, you know, things like that. But other than that, you know, it's . . . that's the only reason I can see why people would use a gun.

A few inmates who had been incarcerated for long periods argued that guns do not provide any protection. Instead, protection comes from the way a person "projects himself." In the context of prison life, where successfully projecting an image of potential violence may mean the difference between being a victim and being respected, this kind of answer makes sense. This is especially true of several inmates who said that they simply would overpower another person carrying a gun at some point when the gun possessor did not expect an attack. For instance, Renato, who had been incarcerated for 17 years, argues that a gun simply will not protect someone.

RENATO: Having a gun doesn't make me safe. What makes you safe is yourself, with your mind. That's what makes you safe. If some nut's gonna come up and shoot you, he's gonna come up and shoot you. Don't make any difference whether you have got a gun or not. So there's nothing you can do about it, you can't stop lightning, you can't stop psychopaths, you know, from happening. Then again, this poor old man that I killed . . . I mean, he could have had all the guns in the world and I'd have, I'd have . . . you know, I'm like a bolt of lightning. There's no containing a bolt of lightning.

Trent, another inmate incarcerated nearly 10 years for murder, goes one step further and argues that weak people carry guns.

TRENT: About 80 percent of the people who carry guns want to be on the street, but can't fight. They want to be thugs, but they can't fight so they'd rather carry guns. When I was growing up, we fought. Now, the thing is to carry a gun. They think they're bad because they're carrying a gun. People think they give them power. All I did was fight.

Thus, for the most part, accounts of gun use among inmates incarcerated over eight years were focused mainly on power, and many talked only about protection to specifically let the interviewer know that it was not an important motivator for obtaining a gun.

Outliers

It is important to point out that some inmates are more likely to take on the "convict" role than others who may resist the prison code and try to keep their nose clean and stay low. Thus, not every inmate will become a convict. Research suggests that, in reality, some offenders take on the role of convict quickly, but others avoid the role for their entire stay (Irwin and Cressey 1962). In line with these observations, several inmates who we interviewed did not fit neatly into the power or protection categories. A few inmates ($n = 5$) reported that neither power nor protection was a reason that people possess guns. Two of these inmates had been incarcerated less than three years, one for five years, and the other two for more than eight years. One inmate was a young woman who killed her boyfriend, three were older white men in their fifties, and one male inmate was convicted in a well-publicized case and claimed innocence. There did not appear to be any discernible pattern among these five inmates who did not mention protection or power as motivators for owning a weapon.

As noted above, the relatively new inmates who mentioned that power was an important reason to carry a gun were likely to have been incarcerated previously for another offense and, therefore, already might have been familiar with the prison culture. One inmate who had been incarcerated less than one year and had no previous prison experience, Miquel, clearly did not talk about protection as a motivating factor for obtaining a gun. Miquel was a gang member who had moved to Denver from the Midwest.

INTERVIEWER: Why do people carry guns?

MIQUEL: Most people that use . . . use weapons is basically a false security. They have, uh . . . they feel that, with a gun, they have control. I mean, that's my opinion. Uh, and that's how I always felt. . . . I was in a place to fight, but it was the fact that I had the upper hand on you because I had more power. But as I grew older, I realized that the . . . the control and the security was like . . . it was . . . it was the power, the sensation that, you know, if you had a gun, it was basically you . . . you were in control.

Although it is not possible to account for Miquel's statements, he clearly is unlike the majority of relatively new incarcerated inmates who argued that protection is one of the more important motivating factors for possessing a gun.

Among the more experienced inmates, four did not fit any categories. These four inmates argued that protection was an important motivator for obtaining a gun, but power was not. All were men, convicted of murder or attempted murder, and three were severe violent offenders (i.e., they had extensive amounts of criminal violence in their past according to their prison files and their own personal accounts of past crimes). One of the four offenders, who served in the military prior to being incarcerated and did not have a history of violence, argued that people mainly possess guns to hunt and protect their families. Such accounts are not inconsistent with research on the gun-carrying population outside of prison.

Future Gun Possession and Use

Sociologists recognize that socialization is a lifelong process in which individuals develop in particular circumstances (Sampson and

Laub 1993). In prison, the process of socialization or resocialization takes place in a total institution where inmates are isolated from the rest of society. The interviews that we conducted with inmates convinced us that the prison culture is dominated by the inmate/prison code (Sykes and Messinger 1960). Consistent with these interviews, the inmate code can be described as resting largely on "exaggerated images of masculinity by encouraging 'macho' behavior while condemning perceived weakness" (Welch 1996). As inmates become more exposed to the inmate code, they come to understand the rules and expectations that guide the behavior in prison. Findings about the motivations for gun possession suggest that the prison culture is internalized in the attitudes and beliefs about the world as shaped by prison life. That is, an inmate's personality is shaped by his or her social circumstances.

The interviews provided us with evidence to support the position that inmates incarcerated for longer periods of time are more likely than those incarcerated for shorter periods to describe power as the primary reason that others possess guns. This may be attributed to early prison experiences where the norms of prison life are alien to novice inmates. As several older inmates suggest, new inmates need to be taught the correct view of the world. In such a setting, prison violence often may be viewed by the newly arrived inmate as highly unpredictable. In such a context, it is not surprising that inmates frequently become consumed with thoughts about how they can avoid becoming victims. Thus, inmate accounts of why people are motivated to possess guns are likely to be shaped by their own fear and uncertainty, and why they report that self-protection is the most important reason that others have for possessing guns. However, we also were interested in speculating on whether these inmate perceptions about why people carry guns impact inmates' thoughts about whether they would carry guns when released from prison. It should be noted here that most of the inmates who we interviewed were facing several more years of incarceration (three had life sentences) and perhaps were too far away from release to imagine life outside of prison as a real possibility. Thus, they may have been boastful about their likelihood of possessing or using a gun again in the future. Perhaps, too, questions about living on the outside caused inmates to simply revert to their preprison personality (see Irwin and Cressey 1962; Jacobs 1974). More likely their answers reflect the conditions outside to which they will eventually return.

Initially, when we asked inmates to estimate whether they could see themselves possessing or using guns again in the future, we expected them to answer "never under any circumstances" or "yes, because the prison system made me crazy." For instance, Russ fit our stereotypical image of what an incarcerated violent gun offender would say when trying to preserve his image as being rehabilitated.

INTERVIEWER: Do you see any situation, then, where you would actually get a gun?

RUSS: No.

INTERVIEWER: Can you see any situation where you would use a gun at all?

RUSS: No. No more guns 'cause I know that guns destroyed my life. Actually, I destroyed my life by using the gun. You know, we all went pulling the gun, you know? But the gun don't fire by itself. And so . . . but, uh . . . no, I don't even want guns for sports. I don't want guns for hobbies. I don't want . . . I . . . I just think they're bad, you know. . . . I hate guns.

On the other hand, Trent fit our stereotypical image of an inmate who was destroyed by the system and is bound to carry a gun again when he leaves prison.

INTERVIEWER: That first time you went to the penitentiary for beating that guy up, you got out. Do you think that did anything to your willingness to carry a gun?

TRENT: No. For the most part I was angry. I had a right to whoop that dude's ass for pulling a knife on me. . . . So I came out of the penitentiary angry. And with that anger built inside me, I know that it's there, and drinking it's bound to come out. That's probably why I beat that dude up—because of all that anger. That's probably why me and my wife argued. I had a lot of built-up anger in me because I was forced to take a four-year prison sentence for some shit that I was really innocent about. I'm still angry about that to this day because they used that against me again for this case to get me a longer sentence. I'm still angry.

However, most inmates who we interviewed were not at all like Russ and Trent. We found that nearly half of all inmates, who could realistically answer the question about whether they would possess a gun again in the future, said that they would possess a gun. In general, most of these inmates felt that a gun was needed for protection.

Figure 4.2 sums up the various reasons that inmates gave for having access to a gun when released from prison. As this figure suggests, most inmates who indicated they would carry a gun again in the future would do so to protect themselves, their property, or their family. Several inmates also said that they would possess a gun to go hunting. Finally, only a few inmates said that they needed a gun to commit crimes. The interviews did not suggest that willingness to possess a gun when released from prison was related to the length of incarceration. Moreover, it was relatively easy for most inmates to imagine a situation where gun possession is necessary. Their main fear was that others would try to use a gun against them or harm them in some way so they would need to be armed to fend off the attacker. For instance, Claude points out that he will certainly carry a gun in the future.

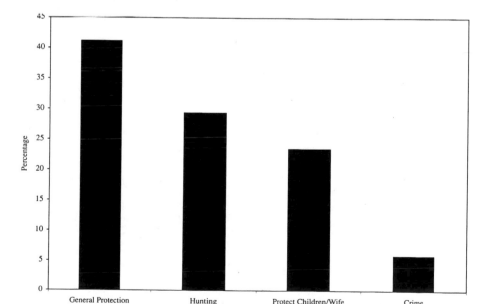

Figure 4.2 Reasons Inmates Give for Possessing a Gun When Released from Prison (n = 17)

INTERVIEWER: Do you think being in prison has had any effect on your willingness to carry a gun in the future?

CLAUDE: Me? I've kind of changed my life. I can't say I'm not going to carry a gun and I can't say that I will carry a gun.

INTERVIEWER: Under what situations do you see yourself perhaps using a gun?

CLAUDE: When I think of myself, if I do not carry a gun in [city], you know, ah, somebody is going to try to kill me. You know, in [state], I wouldn't carry a gun. But other people, you know, they might have. I don't know man, I just . . . I am just the type of person that I probably will carry a gun. You know I not going to go out for some punk, you know, on the street. If he's going to kill me, he's going to have to work for it.

Isaiah also says that he will carry a gun for protection when he is released.

ISAIAH: I think that, yeah, I would definitely carry a gun again [inaudible] because it was such a part of my life for such a long time. I just don't see no foreseeable reason why I would want to carry one.

INTERVIEWER: Can you think of any situations where you might feel that you would have to use a gun again?

ISAIAH: Only to protect myself and my family.

Other inmates who said that they needed a gun for protection, however, also claimed that they would never carry a gun again but may use one in the proper circumstances. For instance, Newton, who was serving his ninth year of a 22-year sentence for manslaughter, argues that people carry and use guns for protection and power. Newton, like Claude and Isaiah, says that he will never use a gun again unless his life is in danger.

INTERVIEWER: When do you think that guns should be used?

NEWTON: If you feel, in your heart, that your life is about to be taken, then you must provide by using what is necessary. If you think that a gun is your only way out and is your only option. If I knew then what I know now, I could of avoided that situation. A person breaking into your home and threatening your life, invading your space . . . that is the only way I can see to use a gun.

Newton's strategy for avoiding gun use is to manage the situation where a gun might be desirable. On the other hand, Wade, who also felt that people carry guns for reasons of power and protection, argues that he will never carry a gun again and will try to avoid guns at all cost.

WADE: I have three more years. I got a double sentence, but they dropped my sentence now because, in my case, there are so many leaking holes with their witnesses. I got a good chance of getting out early.

INTERVIEWER: Because you've been in prison now, does that affect your willingness to carry a gun in the future?

WADE: I'm not going to carry a gun. I'm not going to hang out with people who does. I'm going to go back out there and get my life straight, and take care of my kids. Make sure they're right when they grow up.

Finally, many of the more experienced inmates who talked about guns as symbols of power expressed that they would not carry a gun, but could see the need to use one and would like one close by "just in case." For example, Chance notes that he likes the protection that guns offer him, but is conflicted when asked about whether he would try to obtain a gun.

INTERVIEWER: Once you get out, you know, can you see any situations where you'd want to carry a gun with you?

CHANCE: I don't see no situation but, if I had a situation and my life was in danger, I could see me picking one up. You know what I'm sayin'?

INTERVIEWER: What kind of situation?

CHANCE: It could be a life-threatening situation. I don't like guns just like the next person. You know what I mean? I don't like to carry them. I don't like them around, you know? But I like to be able to reach out and get one anytime something like that happens. To be truthful, I like to be able to reach, you know?

INTERVIEWER: So you'd like to own one just in case?

CHANCE: Yeah. No, I mean, I like to know somebody that have one and I be able to reach. I don't like that, man. That's for real. Because I really feel if you have 'em around, you're gonna eventually use it.

INTERVIEWER: And . . . and in what situations do you think you'd use it?

CHANCE: Some dude just hits you or something. And you got a pistol. You would shoot him. You know? 'Cause you like, hey, I don't have to fight this cat. I don't have to fight this mountain lion, you know? I don't have to run. I can just point it at him and shoot him. You know?

Discussion

Research on the impacts of prisonization has declined significantly in recent years "perhaps because many studies have failed to substantiate the basic tenets of the prisonization hypothesis" (Walters 2003:401). Although our observations suggest that inmates' attitudes about why people carry guns may change in prison, it does not appear that inmates connect these perceptions to their own behavior. Many inmates claimed that the crime for which they were convicted was committed with a gun that was carried for self-protection. If recently released inmates believe that others are carrying guns for expressive reasons (to show power), it could increase the probability that they would possess a gun for protection (Blumstein 1995a, 1995b). This finding concerned us greatly because it suggests that the inmates who we interviewed may make choices that will put them in a situation similar to the one that caused them to go to prison in the first place.

We found that incarceration is not likely to deter inmates from imagining a situation where they would like to own a gun again in the future. Nearly all those who we interviewed told us that they could obtain guns readily when on the outside, and we believe them. Moreover, most inmates said that they would like to own or have access to a gun again for purposes of protection. These statements were relatively consistent among inmates who viewed guns as symbols of power or protection, and both power and protection. When framed in this way—and given the interviewees' accounts of gun use presented in Chapter 2—it is clear that those inmates unknowingly may create a situation that would cause them to commit a future gun crime that would send them back to prison. In short, the interviews suggest that prison changes inmates' views about guns from being symbols of protection to being symbols of power. However, it does not appear that this change in attitude increases or decreases an inmate's beliefs about his or her propensity to possess a gun when released from prison. Antwan, a 32-year-old serving 12 years for his violent gun offense, nicely sums up this reality as follows.

ANTWAN: I'm at the point to where, in here I have to survive and, you know, you never know when you might have to hurt somebody in here just to make sure. And it's just like, you know, with that frame of mind going and going, if they let me out now, you know, I'll still be in that frame of mind—of survival. And they do it to people everyday. One of my good buddies just got out yesterday and he's been in this survival mode this whole time, and all of a sudden he's out on the street and he's still in survival mode. It's hard to change your ways.

INTERVIEWER: So do you see yourself carrying a gun?

ANTWAN: Yeah. It would be a matter of months, I think, and then I would.

Sadly, if inmates like Antwan who say they would possess a gun when released from prison do obtain that gun, they likely will find themselves in a situation similar to the one that caused them to be classified as a violent gun offender.

The issues discussed in this chapter represent a moment in time for the offenders who we interviewed. Instead of looking only backward at their criminal behavior as in Chapters 2 and 3, these inmates evince a time shift here in that they recollect the reasons why guns were important in the past, what they think these weapons represent now in the course of incarceration, and how they conceive of the situation when they will return to their communities some time in the future. The shift in time orientation will continue in Chapter 5 where we consider the interviewees' views on a new gun law that did not exist during their time on the outside, but may nevertheless affect their behavior after they are released.

5

Changing Concealed Carry Laws

A WAVE OF NEW GUN LAWS ACROSS THE UNITED STATES HAS liberalized the possession of concealed weapons. Utter defines *concealed carry gun laws* as providing "for the issuance of carrying concealed weapons licenses, which allow individuals to bear loaded, hidden weapons on their persons" (2000:67). This legislation is meant to reduce crime by forcing criminals to contend with the possibility that potential victims may be carrying concealed weapons. One type of concealed weapons law is known as "shall issue."

Shall issue includes "laws that direct law enforcement officials to issue 'concealed carry' weapons licenses to anyone who applies, unless the person is disqualified for some designated reason, such as having been convicted of a felony" (Utter 2000:67). Other restrictions may include minimum age, mental health history, and required training. A total of 37 states (or 74 percent of the US states) currently have undisputed shall-issue laws, with most of them extending the right to nonresidents as well. Colorado is one state that has made the move to a shall-issue law.

Research on the concealed carry laws suggests that patterns of gun ownership are not likely to change as a result of the passage of such laws (Kleck 1997). That is, shall-issue laws are likely to legalize what was previously illegal for those individuals willing to go through the permitting process. Thus, the impact of these gun laws on crime is likely inconsequential (Kleck 1997). Similarly, Kleck and

Tark (2004) also find, based on National Crime Victimization Survey data, that the defensive use of guns is likely to actually reduce victimization (see also Kohn 2004). Although we, as researchers, are aware that gun laws are not likely to impact crime rates in a meaningful way, the gun offenders who we interviewed were highly interested in shall-issue policies. In fact, several inmates brought up concealed weapons and shall-issue policies as topics of interest that needed to be discussed. Thus, at the same time that we recognize discussing concealed weapons permits was important to inmates, we also acknowledge that inmates' views may not reflect empirical evidence on Colorado's shall-issue policy.

In contrast to Chapters 2, 3, and 4, where the interviewees look inward and backward about their behavior, the focus in this chapter is more external and, to a large extent, hypothetical in that we are asking them to speculate about what impact the law might have in hopes of gaining some insight into their views and beliefs about guns and gun use. Rather than focus on the controversial nature and extensive literature associated with shall-issue legislation, we focus primarily on the reaction of the inmates to this legislation.

Shall-Issue Concealed Carry Gun Law

In 2003, Colorado enacted a law that codified a shall-issue policy regarding the issuance of permits for carrying concealed weapons by its county sheriffs. Essentially, the bill (Senate Bill 03-024) that led to the law (Section 18-12-2 of the Colorado Revised Statutes) noted that inconsistencies existed among jurisdictions within Colorado concerning concealed carry and that this led to public uncertainty about varying rules and their application. Because Colorado had an interest, given the importance of self-defense, in no citizen being denied a concealed carry weapon and in ensuring statewide consistency, this resulted in the state having to impose its definitions and criteria for issuing such permits on local jurisdictions. Although a few minor criteria have been omitted here, the law requires county sheriffs to issue such a permit to an applicant who is a Colorado resident; is at least 21 years of age; is not a chronic alcohol abuser; is not a user of or addicted to drugs; is not a convicted criminal; does not have a restraining order in place against him or her; and has demonstrated, through documentary evidence, competence in the use of a handgun.

In addition, the law allows individuals to carry guns without concealed carry permits in an automobile and for hunting purposes; requires sheriffs to maintain a confidential database of those issued permits; and provides for judicial review of permit denials, suspensions, and revocations. The law effectively repealed the "may-issue" provisions under which Colorado previously operated.

From a social policy perspective, shall-issue concealed carry laws incorporate the following features (see Theodoulou and Kofinis 2004). First, the state involves itself in an *action*, in contrast to inaction, to bring about a particular outcome: that of loosening and substituting for whatever local restrictions, such as qualifications or applicant characteristics, may exist. Second, the *formal players* or legislators, by enacting concealed carry legislation, have chosen to side with one set of *informal players* or claims-makers (i.e., those who argue that restrictions on gun ownership and transport should be loosened versus those who would like to keep them more stringent). Third, on the surface, enacting shall-issue concealed carry laws appears to be a change in procedural policy (i.e., it changes how such permits are to be issued). At the same time, it clearly has substantive implications in that a larger group of individuals than under the previous legal requirements benefits in being able to carry concealed firearms. Fourth, these laws are mostly distributive in that specific individuals—those wanting to carry concealed weapons—benefit from the change as opposed to redistributive policies that benefit one group while shifting resources to them from others. Kopel adds, "Of course, everyone is a potential beneficiary of 'concealed carry' reform. Since criminals do not know which of their potential victims may be armed, even persons without carry permits would enjoy increased safety from any deterrent effect" (1996:11). (See also Lenzen 1995.) Fifth, shall-issue laws tend more toward being self-regulatory (i.e., eligible individuals should be allowed to carry concealed weapons) as opposed to being regulatory (i.e., where the government entity decides who is eligible for carrying concealed weapons). Finally, although such laws may appear to be material policies (i.e., they provide a tangible benefit to an individual in the form of the concealed weapon that he or she may carry legally), they also are symbolic in the sense that they provide the official backing of the state for an expansive view of guns in American society. For example, Jiobu and Curry, using General Social Survey data, show that "individuals with little faith in the three branches of the federal government are more likely to own firearms than individuals with higher levels of confidence" consistently over time (2001:77). The laws being discussed here serve to symbolically support low confidence in the responsibility of governmental entities for the safety and protection of individual citizens. They suggest instead that individuals should assume greater responsibility for ensuring their own safety.

Lott argues that the basis for shall-issue laws comes primarily from deterrence theory, couched in terms of the risks and rewards or the costs and benefits of concealed carry as opposed to "open carry" of guns.

> The case for allowing concealed handguns—as opposed to openly carried handguns—relies on this argument. When guns are concealed, criminals are unable to tell whether the victim is armed before striking, which raises the risk to criminals committing many types of crimes. On the other hand, with "open carry" handgun laws, a potential victim's defensive ability is readily identified which makes it easier for criminals to choose the most vulnerable prey. (2006:271)

In contrast to Lott's arguments, some researchers have argued that the main rationale for the passage of shall-issue laws is to provide citizens with a means of self-defense (Kleck 1991). That is, the purpose of these laws is to disrupt crimes, not deter them from taking place.

In addition to reasons based on philosophical or political predilections (Kopel 1996) and legalistic arguments (Lenzen 1995), the contention that shall-issue concealed carry policies disrupt crimes, which forms the crux of the argument for shall-issue concealed carrying of guns, should be verified by direct questioning of offenders who have been involved in violent events involving guns. That is to say, we should test the central behavioral supposition underlying this policy by asking violent gun offenders regarding their own thinking. The perspectives of gun offenders have direct relevance to the debate about a policy that allows law-abiding citizens greater access to these weapons. This chapter examines the viewpoints and thoughts of offenders who have used guns for committing crimes in connection with a policy that makes it easier for citizens (i.e., potential victims) to carry concealed weapons: Colorado's shall-issue policy regarding the issuance of permits for carrying concealed weapons.

Some of the issues we explore in this chapter are whether inmates report that shall-issue concealed carry provisions make it more likely for those contemplating criminal actions to acquire weapons, and whether they report that they are likely to be deterred by the possibility that those they confront during the commission of a crime are likely to be carrying concealed weapons.

In contemplating such issues, it would be useful to examine the views of those who have gone through the process of thinking about and carrying through with violent criminal behavior. Wright and Rossi (1986, 1994) were the first to study the larger topic of felons (drawn from various prisons) and guns by asking them whether they had used guns in committing their offenses. However, they did not delve into their thought processes regarding calculations, if any, that led up to the violent event, and their views on the role of guns in such events. The views of gun offenders on shall-issue gun policies are particularly important for two reasons. First, the policy is based on assumptions regarding the thinking and behavior of these individuals, their viewpoints, and their projected reactions. Second, after such laws are passed, it is these individuals who will interpret the actions of others who may or may not be carrying concealed weapons and align their subsequent actions accordingly. Unfortunately, previous research on the topic of carrying concealed weapons has not focused on those who have such personal knowledge.

Asking Inmates About Shall-Issue Concealed Carrying

Below is an example that typifies how we asked an inmate about Colorado's shall-issue law if the inmate did not bring it up on his or her own.

INTERVIEWER: You've heard about that new concealed weapon law that the Colorado legislature passed?
INTERVIEWEE: Yes, I've heard about that.
INTERVIEWER: What do you think about it?

Variations of the last question (e.g., "What are your thoughts about the new law?" or "Do you support or oppose the new law? Tell us why.") were used depending on the conversational context, the interviewer, and the interviewee. We then listened to answers that the inmates gave regarding their opinions of the shall-issue law and probed for further explanations as needed (e.g., "Why do you think so?" "Why does carrying a concealed gun increase your feeling of protection?" "How is the new law going to increase/reduce crime?"). We acknowledge that minor variations in questioning may have resulted in slightly different responses from the interviewees, but the overall focus was always on determining their views about and reactions to the change in the concealed carry policy.

Although all the interviewees were in prison and therefore cut off from the larger society, they were surprisingly well aware of the shall-issue policy. This topic came up during the course of 40 (of the 73) interviews. In fact, 37 of the 40 inmates in this subsample had heard about the law. Of these 40 inmates, 14 supported the law and 22 were against it; 4 either were not sure or had no opinion on the topic. This split, with the majority of inmates opposed to concealed carrying policies, is generally consistent with public opinion (see Hemenway, Azrael, and Miller 2001; Smith 2002).

We categorize the interviewees' responses to the inquiries on concealed carry weapons policy as follows. First, we consider the degree of positive and negative opinions among the inmates on the new less-restrictive concealed carry policy enacted in Colorado. Second, we assess the reasons given for each viewpoint. Third, we summarize the major themes that are presented underlying each viewpoint.

Findings

We found that most inmates who we talked with were against the shall-issue law. Of course, this finding is not surprising because these inmates would not be allowed to carry guns legally when released from prison. Thus, they would gain nothing as a result of this change in the laws. Yet we were surprised to learn that some inmates actually supported the law. We were curious to understand the reasons that inmates provided (i.e., how they explained, justified, or rationalized the position they took) for their positive or negative views of the shall-issue legislation. What follows is a description of those views.

Positive Views of Shall Issue

We found that inmates who agreed with the less-restrictive law on issuing concealed weapons permits represented a minority of the interviewees. However, their reasons for supporting the shall-issue policy in Colorado fell into two general categories: (1) those inmates who believed that the policy would deter crime and therefore reduce the crime rate, and (2) those inmates who argued that the policy would help individuals protect themselves.

Deterrence. Some inmates who supported shall issue thought that the policy would increase the number of people carrying guns and that this would produce a deterrent effect. For example, Carlo, a 38-year-old man convicted of murder, argues that, "it is pretty hard to rob somebody who is armed." He talks of the possibility of a robbery victim possessing a gun during a robbery, and says that it would cause him to have doubts about selecting a potential crime target.

Thus, we find agreement by some inmates with the concealed weapons law for its possible deterrent effect, but they also emphasize the importance of knowing how to handle the weapon. As Newton explains, "If you're properly educated about carrying a firearm, I have no problem. I am pretty much for it." Newton also feels that the law would serve a deterrent purpose if it promotes gun carrying among the general population.

INTERVIEWER: Do you think that, if someone carries a gun, a potential robber might be deterred?

NEWTON: Yes. They'll leave him alone and go to the ones that don't have a weapon. But these days, females are carrying just as much. And the jackers are going to start losing, but they better start waking up.

INTERVIEWER: So it will reduce the numbers of robberies?

NEWTON: It will reduce the number of robberies. Once they see on the news that a robber is shot and killed by a citizen, that's going to scare them. The jackers are going to start thinking twice.

Isaiah, who had been convicted of armed robbery, believes that the shall-issue law will have a deterrent effect. Again, Isaiah emphasizes that being trained in the proper use and handling of guns is important. We found this theme (gun safety) to be somewhat of a contradiction because all of the inmates in this sample had been convicted of a violent offense with a firearm. However, many of the interviewees grew up with and around weapons, especially those from rural areas like Isaiah, who had been exposed to gun safety precautions. Isaiah notes, "I think that, the more people that carry guns, people like you, just common people that carry weapons—that are educated about them, that know how to use them, will keep crime down." Isaiah then goes on to explain that average citizens carrying concealed handguns under the shall-issue policy might have deterred him from committing his most recent robbery. For Isaiah, the chance that a potential victim may be in possession of a firearm would certainly affect his decision to commit a robbery. He says, "It will keep crime down, because I wouldn't have gone into that A&W store if I had known there was a good chance that one in five people in that store would have been carrying a handgun. They probably would have shot me."

When probed further concerning the concealed weapons law's deterrent capability, Isaiah goes on to visualize a scenario in which someone shoots him in the act of a robbery. Here, he expresses his fear and uncertainty of not knowing whether the victim could be armed, resulting in harm to himself. This explains why he believed that the shall-issue policy is a deterrent for confrontational criminal activity.

> ISAIAH: I think it would deter . . . you know someone is shooting up the store [based on the movie *Zero Factor* he once saw], and somebody shoots them or attacks them while they are robbing the store. You know, if everybody has the right to carry a handgun and you know going into the store, you are going to think about that above anything. You might have your plans all set up, and you'll be like, "Well, what if I am standing there holding up the clerk and the guy behind me sitting in a chair shoots me in the back?"

Isaiah's views echo many of the same ideas as the policymakers and researchers who argue that carrying guns will ultimately deter crime (Kopel 1996). Windord who was convicted of assault with a gun, put it this way, "I think, I think, well a lot of people that do [rob people] are not too smart so they may not think about it [whether victim might have gun] at first, but I think it would [deter]. If, if, if I was gonna rob somebody and I thought maybe they had a gun, I think I would be more cautious about it."

Related to notions of deterrence, other inmates perceive the concealed carry law as influencing their interpersonal interactions with those who are seen as threatening to them physically. In this view, the perpetrator's behavior toward others, in both offensive and defensive postures, is affected directly by the uncertainty of the targeted victim's probability of having a concealed weapon. For instance, Patrick, a 28-year-old convicted of robbing an individual at gunpoint, explains the danger to the perpetrator if the potential victim is carrying a gun.

> PATRICK: It could have a good impact as far as people acting in society 'cause you never know who is going to be packing and who is not. So if you can't see a gun, you know, you're going to stay on your p's and q's, you know. You're always going to be wondering "I better keep in line" 'cause you never know if a person might be carrying a weapon. You may try to rob a woman in a parking lot, but she might be having a handgun.

This propensity of another to hide a gun on his or her person was a factor that some proponents of the concealed carry law perceived as a functional deterrent to physical altercations between conflicting parties. For example, Claude, who killed another gang member who disrespected him, notes, "Nobody is going to pick on a person that has a gun. That's the way I see it."

Protection. Wright and Rossi (1994:14–15) found that self-protection and the possibility that a victim might be armed were the main reasons that gun offenders obtained guns. In other words, some of the inmates we talked with expressed the desirability of the shall-issue policy in terms of their need for self-protection from those who pose a personal threat to their safety. Darrel put it this way, using the example of a Good Samaritan grandfather.

> DARREL: You know, I know my grandpa, he used to carry a .410 shotgun behind the seat and a .38 underneath the seat. He's a Good Samaritan. I don't care how good of a Samaritan you are, in today's world, if somebody is pulled over with a flat tire and you get out to help them change a tire, you don't know who's hiding in the bushes. If you have a .38 Snubnose in your pocket as you walk up to ask them if they need help, they never have to know you have that weapon. If you have no malice intent towards them whatsoever except to help them change that tire, you're just protecting yourself to a higher level.

Reed, for example, perceives that he could be victimized, and offers a defensive account for the need to carry concealed weapons. He explains, "I have applications for carrying a concealed weapon because of my employment. I had situations where I had terminated employees and I felt I would like to have the security of carrying a weapon because of the threats that were made on my life." Reed goes on to say that in his view the new shall-issue policy is a personal decision and that people should decide for themselves whether to carry guns. "But as far as concealed weapons for people to carry them, the qualifications to carry and the training that is required by the state, I think that is the individual's choice."

Once again, we hear that citizens who wish to obtain a gun should possess knowledge regarding gun safety and meet state-mandated qualifications for gun ownership. This subtheme was prevalent among the inmates in this sample who supported the concealed carry law. What we find interesting is how these gun proponents express a genuine belief that it is important for a person to have knowledge about guns and the harm they can cause to others. Yet each study subject had caused serious injury or death to their victim by using a firearm in some altercation, thereby leading to their incarceration. This is not to imply that their desire for operational knowledge of proper gun possession and use is disingenuous, but rather to note the failure to reconcile their gun safety beliefs with their own violent gun behavior.

Negative Views of Shall Issue

The majority of interviewed inmates viewed the Colorado shall-issue law negatively, and thought that it was not going to have any deterrent effect on crime or interpersonal disputes involving guns. In fact, those with negative opinions were adamant in their statements regarding opposition to the policy. Although their perceptions of what may occur in the future varied, all believed such a policy would have the opposite effect of that intended by this legislation. That is, allowing the average citizen to carry a concealed weapon would result in even more harm in the long run.

Increased crime. Some interviewees, like Wiley, believed that the crime rate would increase as a result of more people carrying concealed weapons.

WILEY: I think it could only increase crime. A gun is power and that's why a lot of people have them. You know what I mean? Not everybody is running around with a gun so, if you have a gun, you have the edge on anyone. The police have an edge on us because we don't have as many guns as they do. You know, so they're quicker to pull their gun out and legally use.

Maryland, a 26-year-old woman convicted of several armed robberies, explained further.

MARYLAND: I believe that it [shall issue] is going to make gun crime and crime period increase due to the fact that, if everyone has a gun, anyone can use it. I mean, even if you're never sure if this person is coming to harm you, you can turn around and use your gun when you're certified to have a gun. So I do believe that it is going to make crime, especially with guns, increase.

Wiley and Maryland clearly perceive that there will be more interpersonal violence between conflicting parties if a greater number of people are carrying concealed weapons.

Thad, a 29-year-old who was convicted of aggravated assault for using a gun during an altercation with another person, believes that more people carrying guns will lead to the increased use of them.

THAD: I think it will make more crimes because, if a Person A pulls out a gun on Person B, then Person B will pull out his gun and that will just be worse. The person who is robbing doesn't intend to use it, only to scare people into giving them their stuff. But the person with the certificate to carry a gun will use it to kill because that is their purpose.

According to Thad, when both the criminal and the victim have a gun during an armed robbery, it possibly could turn into a murder because both parties are armed and willing to use their weapons when threatened. Thus, he believes that the new shall-issue law would increase the homicide rate. Similarly, Wade, a 27-year-old convicted of murder, argues that the shall-issue law is likely to increase the homicide rate, "I don't really know. It has been so long since I've been on the streets. The only thing I can really say is that they shouldn't legalize guns and concealed weapons. You can have them in your house but not carry them around, that's not a good thing, because the murder rate in Colorado is going to go up."

Lastly, the belief that concealed weapons will cause more crime, especially violent criminal activity, is presented below. Again, these interviewees foresee an increase in the crime rate directly attributable to a simultaneous increase in the purchase and carrying of concealed weapons by community members. When asked specifically why the homicide rate would go up after the shall-issue law went into effect, many inmates argued that they would be more likely to use deadly force on the street. Trent sums up this position.

TRENT: If I'm on the streets and I know people are carrying concealed weapons, I'll just walk up right to you and shoot you in the head and then take what you have. That way, you don't have a chance to take out your concealed weapon and shoot me. If I'm going to take a chance with my life, I'm going to help my chance and shoot you. That's how some people will think.

Lance also believes that homicide will increase if people start carrying guns as a result of the shall-issue law.

INTERVIEWER: What about this new shall-issue law? What do you think about it?

LANCE: First of all, they only carry a gun if they are afraid of getting hurt. That means hairpin trigger uses. That's never good.

INTERVIEWER: So how would it impact on you while you are pulling these robberies?

LANCE: It can get somebody killed. If I was there and someone pulled a gun, it's on. I'm all armed and mine's already out, and it's loaded. I didn't come there with a fake gun or a plastic gun. I came there with a real gun, and I know how to use it. If somebody goes for a gun, I'm shooting him and I'm not trying to bullshit you. Somebody standing in line trying to be a hero might get everybody shot. I don't think it's a good idea at all for people to have guns. It's better if I'm coming into that store robbing and everybody is unarmed. Nobody is ever going to get hurt. If somebody pulls out a gun, every innocent is subject to get hit.

Although most of our interviewees did not want the public carrying around guns for defensive purposes, they said that having a gun in the home is acceptable. In fact, as we indicated in Chapter 3, many inmates would like to have access to a gun to protect themselves and their family when released from prison. As demonstrated in Chapter 3, the idea that a gun is needed to protect one's family was a recurring theme throughout our interviews. However, none of the interviewees mentioned the problem of gun use in the home during domestic alter-cations or accidental shootings by children who have access to guns within the home. For instance, Francesco, a 27-year-old convicted of murder, argues, "I'm fine with it in the home. Having that helps to protect your family and that type of thing. But as far as out in the streets and concealed and stuff like that, I don't think people should do it because there are many more chances that people will start pulling them out on other people." Russ, a 43-year-old convicted of murder, sees more injuries with more guns in the hands of lawful citizens.

RUSS: But I feel people getting hurt with guns is really gonna increase with the new law they just passed. You're gonna have more honest people buying guns. Now, you're gonna have more out there guys like me. If I knew these good people work hard, go to church, go on vacations, and I know they are gone with guns in the house, I will get them [guns].

Russ perceives an increase in the theft of guns from households as a result of the increase in noncriminal ownership of firearms due to the shall-issue law. Wade had a similar outlook on the movement of guns from noncriminals to criminals, but presents a different rationale for being in opposition to the new gun policy. Wade predicts that non-criminal community members will sell guns more frequently, "You got people who can get guns legally and then can sell them on the streets to people doing felonies. They are going to put the guns right back on the street."

The interviews suggest that several inmates, who had not been able to purchase firearms legally because of state and federal back-ground checks, had indeed purchased firearms with the knowledge and help of others who were able to pass the background checks (straw buys). We did not find any evidence that legitimate gun own-ers sold their weapons on the street for a profit. However, this finding does not include gun show sales where some inmates said that anyone could purchase a firearm without a background check. We should be clear, however, that only 0.7 percent of gun felons surveyed in a 1997 report obtained their weapons at gun shows, according to the Bureau of Justice Statistics (Harlow 2001). Nevertheless, this perception is important at least in terms of where some felons are likely to attempt to buy guns.

Interaction of more guns with gangs, alcohol and drug abuse, and mental states. Several interviewees provided other categories of answers regarding the behavioral implications of the shall-issue law. That is to say, they presented multiple reasons why the law is faulty. Thus, we examine various inmate perceptions of what the shall-issue law will produce when it intersects with gang membership, poor mental health, and alcohol and drug abuse. Frederic, a 25-year-old gang member convicted of aggravated assault with a gun, claims that the law will lead to more gang members preemptively possessing guns, based on his individual assessments of dispute situations.

FREDERIC: Bad idea, everybody can use a gun. I was 18 when I got my first gun. A lot of situations start out as a dispute. What happens in between? For instance, another gang member comes up and wants to beat you up. You can't let things slide. The one way you are going to eliminate conflict is to kill people. You're going to shoot me, I'm going to shoot you first.

In this situation, Frederic is simply assuming that every rival gang member is carrying a handgun. Thus, he believes he must be violent and preemptive and shoot his rival quickly. In sum, according to Frederic, the more people carry guns, the greater the likelihood those guns will be used in gang conflicts.

Johnathan, a 60-year-old convicted of aggravated murder who had used alcohol heavily, claims that the drug was a decisive factor in his gun use. For Johnathan, the shall-issue law is likely to increase crime because many people who are likely to possess guns are also likely to abuse alcohol. Johnathan argues that the shall-issue law is "insanity," noting, "You give a man a drink and a gun and tell him this is completely legal and we condone this. . . . I'm sorry, but the thing coming out of the end of the gun is gonna kill you." Along with the distorted mental state that alcohol and drug use may cause, Johnathan argues that the emotional stability of the person abusing intoxicants plays havoc with reasoning. An individual, criminal or noncriminal, carrying a concealed weapon while under the influence of a psychoactive substance and in a heightened emotional state, can lead to disastrous consequences. Indeed, a large majority of violent offenders are found to be using alcohol or drugs or both around the time of their offense (Kuhns 2005). A similar finding emerged in this sample of inmates. Our case files and interviews suggest that almost every inmate was using alcohol or drugs at the time of their crime. Although the shall-issue law specifically prohibits those who abuse alcohol from receiving permits for carrying concealed weapons, these inmates did not see that prohibition as a barrier to obtaining a gun.

Regarding drug and alcohol use, several inmates argued that violence might result when certain emotional states are combined with the possession of firearms. Bob is typical.

BOB: It [the new gun law] probably wouldn't have made a difference because. . . .
INTERVIEWER: But you could get killed!
BOB: You know at the time, when you're on drugs, you're so strung out, nothing matters but to get the drugs. And you do whatever you need to do to get the drugs.

Trent, a 33-year-old convicted of murder, contends that people are more likely to use guns when experiencing multiple emotional problems.

TRENT: Let's say there is an average guy like yourself, say like you get a permit to carry a gun and that you and your wife argue one day. And then you get all crazy, you might want to take out that gun and do something crazy. Or let's just say have a really bad day. You come home, you lost your job and you feel like shooting somebody, you could snap. I'm not saying you will, but it's possible.

Thus, Trent offers a logical consequence for the use of a firearm when anger from experiencing life's typical problems overtakes a person who has immediate access to that weapon. This point is also explained by Wiley, a 22-year-old inmate, who argues that anger combined with the shall-issue law will lead to more illegal gun violence.

WILEY: A gun is power and that's why a lot of people have them. Not everyone is running around with a gun so, if you have a gun, you

115

have an edge on anyone. So it's more of a power thing. . . . When I didn't have a gun and something came up, it gave me that much more time to think about what I was about to do, what I could have done. Reacting to my anger with a gun on you, and a situation occurs, the natural reaction is to use it. With everyone in town running around with a gun, you know, that's going to limit your actions period.

This viewpoint is amplified by Newton.

NEWTON: The people who are issuing these gun [permits] don't know that you can flip out and kill off everything. You can have a stressful day. Anybody can flip out at anytime. Stress is a power killer, it destroys the mind. And hey, everybody has their breaking point. That's the thing with a concealed weapon because they can go into any place and shoot up the place. And then shoot themselves.

In addition, the subject of youth and criminal activity coupled with the attitudinal state of invulnerability to physical harm led several inmates to argue that the shall-issue law will result in disastrous consequences. In a retrospective interpretation of his attitudes toward being harmed and harming others, David, a 33-year-old convicted of attempted murder, provides an insightful view of what he was like as a youth when asked if he would rob again now that many more people will be carrying weapons under the shall-issue law.

DAVID: That's interesting. Would it make a difference if you say this guy could be carrying a gun? The way I was thinking about it back then, I didn't care about anybody or myself for that matter. In the state of mind when I was younger, someone carrying didn't mean a damned thing. It didn't matter. The mentality was that I was super-human—you're not going to kill me.

Related to David's feelings of youthful invulnerability are the responses of other interviewees when probed on the subject of potential harm they might suffer for just possessing a gun. Most of them resorted to a discussion of their unresponsive attitudes toward anyone attempting to change their criminal activities or attitudes when younger. Their position was that nothing could have changed their behavior at that time in their lives. Perhaps, there may be times during a youth's delinquent life history when any intervention may be ineffectual. According to the interviewees, there were periods during adolescence when nothing could have persuaded them to stop carrying a gun or being ready and willing to engage in violent conflict resolution, not even a shall-issue law.

Discussion

The voices represented in this chapter are distinctive for two reasons. First, gun offenders add validity to policy discussions by way of their own past violent experiences and projections of themselves in similar future situations. Second, the lived experiences of these individuals, although relevant to a policy that ostensibly targets the thinking and behavior of offenders (i.e., those who have actually used guns to commit crimes), have largely been ignored in the literature.

As previously noted, several researchers have argued that victimization might decrease due to the offender's perception that there exists a high probability of potential victims being armed (Kopel 1996; Lott 1998). In other words, concealed weapons should prove to be a deterrent in face-to-face violent crime. It must be pointed out that this supposed deterrent effect was the logic, among other factors, cited as a major reason for the passage of the shall-issue legislation. Whether concealed weapons laws deter overall crime or not was not the primary concern of this research. The views of convicted violent gun users toward their future gun use and the use of guns by noncriminal members of the community are, of course, of concern to us. However, it must be noted that most of this sample of convicted gun felons disagreed with the deterrence premise and suggested that concealed carry permits may embolden (Wilcox, May, and Roberts 2006) those carrying guns and thereby provoke violence.

Given that we studied convicted gun offenders, the finding that the majority of the interviewees viewed negatively the change in Colorado's concealed carry gun permit law from may issue to shall issue did not come as a surprise. Many of the inmates in this sample argued that more guns and greater gun availability would result in more violent crime. The laws themselves, most inmates argued, would have little impact on the thinking of potential offenders who are likely to be undeterred because they do not care or because they are already prepared for that eventuality. We were, however, surprised to learn that there were positive opinions regarding Colorado's shall-issue law among several of these "experts" in violent crime. Support for the law was based on the perceived deterrent value of concealed weapons in various situations, and the recognition of the need for self-protection against possible attacks.

In one sense, the reactions of these inmates mirror the larger public split (Smith 2002) and debates regarding concealed carrying of weapons. Thus, several questions emerge from this research. Does a less-restrictive gun permit issuance policy mean that potential offenders will be deterred, or is it likely to have no impact on their thinking when approaching a crime situation? Does the right to self-protection imply that society has to countenance the introduction of more guns into public places (particularly where gang activity and alcohol are also present)? How much potential lethality is deterrent enough in our communities, and how will we know when that point has been reached? The inmates we interviewed were unexpectedly knowledgeable about these debates and enthusiastic about transmitting that knowledge to us.

The inmates in this sample advanced several behavioral and policy-related reasons for their positive and negative viewpoints toward the shall-issue law. If the accounts of these inmates' reactions to the law find some reflection on the street, the law will have little effect on the violent crime rate (Kovandzic and Marvell 2003). The dismissive reaction of several interviewed offenders to the law is likely to be offset by its potential deterrent value that some other inmates described. That is, in many situations, offenders will be more likely to react to potentially armed citizens with deadly force but, in other situations, they will be deterred from such use.

However, we believe that there is also cause for us to question this conclusion that there will essentially be "no change." From the perspective of those who believe in less-restrictive gun policies, it could be argued that it is logical and to be expected that more of these inmates will oppose shall-issue laws and offer arguments consistent with their position because it is in their self-interest to do so. After all, both objectively and as predicted by deterrence theory, the shall-issue law makes the job of robbing or murdering someone more of a risk to these offenders when there is a greater probability that victims possess the ultimate, lethal means of defending themselves.

So we might wonder why some of the inmates who we interviewed would voice support for a shall-issue law if it would make their future criminal activity more difficult. There are two possibilities. First, it may be that individual offenders who have a positive opinion of the concealed carry law view the situation not through the lens of their identities as offenders, but through that of their own potential victimization. Second, it is possible that the supportive inmates think the shall-issue law is likely to have a potential deterrent effect on their own future criminal activity. The question becomes whether this potential benefit for crime reduction is offset by the potential increase for crime severity because offenders may escalate their violent behavior by preemptively using lethal force if they believe that their victims may be armed and dangerous. As previously noted, the shall-issue policy is not likely to have much impact on crime rates despite claims by several inmates that such policy may increase crime.

Having explored a series of interrelated topics and themes pertaining to the role of guns in the lives of the offenders who we interviewed and the criminal violence that they participated in, we turn next to a final summing up of the findings, their implications, and analytic applications in Chapter 6.

6

Conclusion:
Limiting Gun Violence

I N THIS CLOSING CHAPTER OF THE BOOK, WE TAKE UP THREE
major interrelated tasks. First, we summarize and review the major
findings of this study in terms of the research agenda we set for ourselves at the beginning. Rather than rehashing each chapter's conclusions, we illustrate the relevance of the findings for analyzing and
understanding everyday events of criminal violence. Second, we
identify and discuss a series of crosscutting observations and themes
that emerged in the course of previous chapters, but that have not
been commented extensively on hitherto. In the course of that discussion, we also identify future directions for research on gun offenders
and gun violence that came forward from this work. Finally, we present our personal perspectives on the individual gun offenders who
have populated the pages of this book that we gleaned in the course
of investigating aspects of their lives that were shaped by guns, criminal behavior, and violence.

What We Learned About Guns,
Criminal Behavior, and Violence

During the course of this research, we questioned, listened to, and
discussed at length a variety of issues with this sample of 73 incarcerated felons. Although we reported the major analytic content of these

conversations in Chapters 2 through 5, several crosscutting issues and themes have not been discussed or commented on, both by necessity and due to the singular focus of this study on guns and gun use. We identify and expand on them here to provide a more complete sense of some of the other directions that this research has taken us.

Gun Felons: Their Past, Present, and Future

The interviewees, in attempting to converse with us and provide accounts of their behavior, often acted as their own "problem solvers." This is to say that they were interested in identifying, tagging, and providing meaning for their past actions that would comport with their view of themselves in the present and that would help project and align (or realign) their course of action in the future. This activity is a common human endeavor (Bem 1967, 1972), and it should not surprise us that incarcerated felons with time on their hands had thought about these issues and, when given an opportunity through the interviews, discussed them at length.

In considering their own histories of violent behavior and possible neutralizations that would help them account for such to the interviewer, the inmates most commonly proffered the denial of victim justification and defeasibility excuse. The idea that the victim deserved what he or she got, and that the violence did not result from anything willful or intentional on the perpetrator's part, may be reinforced and strengthened in the context of gang culture with its emphasis on standing up to others and making them back down in confrontations. Before coming to prison, the interviewees must also have been comforted by thinking the gunplay that occurred during the criminal event was a means of protecting themselves. While in prison, during the time we interviewed them and perhaps upon further reflection, many of the inmates came to believe that people carry guns to show and feel power. It should be added that, ironically, this shift in belief did not mean that the interviewees would stay away from guns because many of them said they would likely obtain a gun for protective purposes when they return to the community. Thus, attitudinal shifts while in prison about the role of guns in everyday interactions may not presage changes in behavior as these inmates contemplate the future. Also looking to the future, would the possibility of a victim who may be carrying a concealed weapon deter them from gun use? The majority of the interviewees expressed negative views regarding the Colorado concealed carry law that makes the possibility of an armed victim more likely, but implied they were not likely to be so deterred. Consequently, the outlook for the future, based on what these gun offenders told us, is rather pessimistic. They are likely to obtain guns and use them in situations where they confront individuals who "had it coming" regardless of the possibility that those they face might be armed with a concealed weapon. Thus, if these inmates were truthful with us, the idea that they will modify their future criminal behavior because others are armed is not likely.

Recounting Involvement in Violent Incidents

Newman (1979), in the course of attempting to define violence, provides many examples of what would constitute such behavior—ranging from political violence to family violence to lethal violence—but complains about the difficulty in defining the phenomenon. He finally settles on a definition that involves the use of force to gain dominance over another or others. It would be safe to say that the interviewees have had considerable experience with situations of violence, have thought about these events over long periods of time, and have considered their own roles as perpetrators in many of these situations. Perhaps consequently, we found little if any hesitation on their part both in providing examples of their understanding of violence and in acknowledging their own participation in such behavior. Although they offered justifications and excuses for their behavior, talked about how the process of gang socialization played a part in their violence (for the gang members in the sample), shifted their opinions over time regarding the importance of guns as facilitators of violence, and discussed how easier access to concealed weapons may or may not alter behavior patterns in themselves, only three of the interviewees denied their own participation in violent crime.

Why were there no additional inmates who plainly denied any such involvement? We speculate that this may partly be due to our strategy of placing the interviewee's summary rap sheet on the table as we conducted his or her interview. It also may be due to the self-selection of inmates who were willing and eager to talk about their violent behavior with us. In other words, they knew what we were looking for and were prepared to give it to us. However, objectively, there was nothing that prevented a given inmate from denying involvement in any form of illegal violent activity. There are other possibilities. The prison environment, with its emphasis on tagging and responding to an inmate on the basis of the criminal behavior noted in his or her prison folder, may have helped strengthen one aspect of the interviewee's identity (i.e., I am a gun felon). This also may have been reinforced by the interview topics that were mainly about guns and gun use in the commission of violent crime.

To some observers, the ease and fluidity with which the interviewees recounted their acts of violent crime may indicate a fundamental lack of either empathy for their victims (as explained in Chapter 3, denial of victim was the most common justification) or respect for the societal norms that they transgressed. It also may indicate a lack of accountability that should have triggered feelings of regret, shame, and guilt, which would have been conveyed to us in the course of the interviews. Although we did not specifically probe for such expressions of emotion, none of the inmates volunteered them.

The Tide of Methamphetamine-Related Gun Violence

Methamphetamine "accounts for a small percentage of the total number of people affected by drug and alcohol problems" (Covey 2007:40) and, therefore, the inmates in this study were not specifically questioned about methamphetamine involvement. However, several interviewees attributed their violent behavior to methamphetamine use, sales, or both. Approximately 25 percent were involved in methamphetamine use or sales at some point in their life. In addition, a number of inmates reported that they believed their methamphetamine involvement was directly responsible for their use of a gun during the commission of their current offense. Although some of the interviewees worried about the interaction between alcohol and other drugs on the one hand and easier access to carrying concealed weapons (see Chapter 5) on the other, few of them asserted that their violent offenses were directly attributable to involvement with alcohol, marijuana, heroin, cocaine, or crack. Although we do not claim that there is an association between gun violence and methamphetamine use, we do find it interesting that meth came up during the interviews with some frequency. Here are some representative excerpts from the interviews that point to the psychological effects of methamphetamine.

RENATO: As far as I know, I drank all my life . . . and, then, when I got into the Marine Corps, I was introduced to the wonderful world of speed, methamphetamines, and that goes right along with my personality because I am hypersensitive and hyperactive.

ISAIAH: I was smoking weed, but I had been doing that, smoking weed, for the past seven years. But at the time, I was shooting speed . . . on a daily basis. [Before that] I was kind of quiet and I didn't really let things bother me . . . which would be contrary to what I'm here for. But I'm not really a violent person and don't have any other violent offense.

WINDORD: Usually, I had a gun around the house. . . . I would never carry it or anything. Then, I started doing the speed. . . . The speed, it seems—like I said, the only time I got into trouble was when I was on the speed—because you are just not thinking right, you know you're not using your head. You don't realize how screwed up your thinking is, but you are.

In addition to the above accounts that speak to the hypothesized physiological effects of methamphetamine, some of the interviewees also suggested that involvement in the methamphetamine market—as opposed to other illegal drug markets—might increase the probability of violent gun use. For instance, Johnathan notes "The last two times [I got in trouble], there was just more methamphetamines. There is a lot of guns used in drug sales and robberies."

We remain skeptical regarding the interviewees' contentions about methamphetamine use "causing" violent behavior in a physiological sense. This skepticism is due to inaccurate attributions in the politics and media about drugs and crime. Such distortions about the relationship between drugs and crime are widespread in US history. For example, in a chapter titled "The Legend of the Crazed Drug Killer," Brownstein shows that "how marijuana use was connected to violence in the 1930s and how crack cocaine use was linked to violence in the 1980s" were "more firmly grounded in politics than science" (2000:18). However, we are confident in asserting that the linkage between drug use and violence that others (Sommers and Baskin 2006) also have found appears to occur more commonly than can be explained by chance alone and, therefore, merits further and more detailed examination.

In the context of this study's other findings, we wonder if the defeasibility excuse provided by some inmates (see Chapter 2), which holds that the violence that happened was not willful on the part of the offender, can also be implicated when an inmate blames the event on methamphetamine. In effect, those who use this excuse blame the mood-altering substance they had ingested instead of themselves (i.e., "It wasn't me; it was the meth"). Similarly, we may point to the centrality of gang socialization (see Chapter 3) regarding guns in the linkage seen between methamphetamine and violence. Specifically, if gangs are involved in the methamphetamine market and emphasize carrying guns for perceived power-related or protective reasons, would this not increase the odds that violent encounters may ensue? Despite our misgivings about the relationship between methamphetamine use and violence, we believe that there are some reasons to examine this issue further in order to establish if there is a possible pathway from one to the other. We currently are in the process of studying the methamphetamine-violence nexus.

Other Directions

Based on the above discussion, we believe several research lines have opened up as a result of this study. Although we have presented a description of certain important aspects of the offender's perspective on guns, violence, and criminal behavior, other questions remain unanswered. What, for example, is the profile of a violent gun offender? Could we identify offenders among us and intervene early enough in the process as a means to ameliorate the problem? Future researchers might ask offenders directly about their recommendations on how society should deal with gun violence. This is an alternative way of inquiring how the offender could have been prevented from turning out the way that he or she did.

Also needed are follow-up studies of the life trajectories of released inmates who had been incarcerated for gun offenses. Future studies could address issues such as whether these inmates will return to a situation where they are likely to use or feel compelled to use guns again. Although it is possible that many gang members may age out of the gang, and therefore gun-related criminal activity, others may not (see Lasley 1992). Those who do not may go back to their earlier social and geographical contexts where they are likely to use guns again. Drug users, specifically methamphetamine users, are also likely to use again and obtain guns, given their perceptions of the danger surrounding drug buying and selling. Other inmates may never use guns criminally again. How will shall-issue concealed carry policies play into all of the above scenarios? Finally, as a result of their prison experiences, are inmates more or less likely to carry guns when they are released, or is incarceration an episode in their lives that is irrelevant to their future behavior? These are all speculations on our part that, even though they flow directly from this project, require systematic examination in future research on the gun offender and gun violence.

In a more general vein, social scientists may explore the relevance of this study's findings both historically and comparatively. Social historians of violence (Gurr 1989; Lane 1997) may wish to examine some of these issues by utilizing available archival data on the attitudes of both offenders and nonoffenders toward gun violence at various points in history. Similarly, it would be instructive for comparative criminologists and criminal justice scholars (Winterdyk and Cao 2004) to study similar topics in countries where firearms are not as easily available as in the United States and in countries that are not tagged as being "obsessed with crime" (Adler 1983) as is the United States.

Final Thoughts

In researching and writing this book about the violent use of guns in criminal offenses, we came away with lasting impressions on two important subjects. We alluded to these topics in the Preface to this book. First, and most obviously, we were struck by the perceptions that were generated in us regarding both convicted felons who are incarcerated for their acts of violence and their rationale for committing such heinous crimes. Second, we became cognizant of our personal reactions to the faces that were attached to the inmates who we interviewed and briefly came to know. In particular, we learned something about who these men and women were before their involvement in crime and violence, and who they perceived themselves to be while serving a lengthy prison sentence.

All too often, the public as well as researchers learn about the consequences of the actions of gun-using criminals through the media, mainly television news and documentaries or extensive newspaper articles. But rarely do we have the opportunity to meet face-to-face with the people who have committed the unlawful acts about which we shake our heads in bewilderment. We were, however, able to do this through the interview process. Often, when we discussed the crimes of the interviewees, we would recall hearing about their past violent actions in the media and connect those memories to the inmates. Some of the more sensational gun violence occurred near to where some of us reside. This brought about a realization that violent gun crimes are never that far from us, even though most of us perceive that such criminality occurs in settings removed from our everyday lives. We thus became aware of our own vulnerability to victimization and, as a result, tended to probe the interviewees in a more in-depth manner. But even as so-called educated, conventional individuals, we often were at a loss to explain to each other the reflective emotions that we felt during an interview when we learned how geographically close an offender had lived or that he or she had grown up in the very neighborhood where we presently resided.

This realization of the close proximity of serious and damaging violence to our families and friends caused much discussion among us during the trips to and from various Colorado prisons as we sought to understand the reasons underlying these violent events. Perhaps, the one and one-half years that we spent researching, categorizing, analyzing, and writing about the interviewees' stories resulted in greater insight regarding who these inmates really are and why they acted in the violent manner that resulted in their victim's injury or death. In short, we believe that this process enhanced our ability to make sense of the seemingly senseless acts of violent gun use that have been chronicled in this book.

Finally, although there is much more research to be performed in the future, we are thankful to the many social and behavioral scientists who came before us who published their studies of criminal gun violence. Their work allowed us to put the violent behavior of the 73 offenders who we interviewed in a theoretical and discursive context that, we hope, will add to the social and behavioral understanding of guns and violent crime. It also is our wish that this book will provide additional knowledge regarding the often emotional issues surrounding the important issue of violent gun behavior and that other researchers will continue where we left off.

APPENDIX

Sample Methodology, Sample Generalizability, Response Bias, and Subsamples

NALYSTS AT THE COLORADO DEPARTMENT OF CORRECTIONS
used a computer-generated simple random sample to select
approximately 200 inmates who had been convicted of gun-related
violent crimes and, thus, were eligible for inclusion in this study. We
then spent several days reading each inmate's prison file at the
department's headquarters in Colorado Springs to verify that the
inmate had indeed been convicted of a gun-related violent crime and
was currently incarcerated in a state prison. After this initial paper
review, 119 inmates met the study's criteria. During the course of
examining the prison files, we also collected detailed information on
inmates' demographics, previous criminal history, and current
offense. The rap sheets that we compiled provided us with a detailed
(figurative) picture of each inmate, and we were thereby able to
become somewhat acquainted with their background and current situation prior to the face-to-face interviews. The rap sheets also acted as
a validity check of the inmates' accounts.

After we had generated the list of gun felons, we contacted each
inmate's case manager via a letter describing the purpose of the interviews and the dates we planned to visit their facility to talk with the
inmates. The case managers then asked the inmates if they would be
willing to be interviewed about their experiences with guns. We
obtained a list of 119 inmates who told their case manager that they
would consider our request. To increase participation, we offered a

$5.00 incentive to each inmate for their time. We decided on the incentive both because we learned that one national-level survey paid inmates $50.00 for an interview and because the prison staff told us that many inmates would not agree to talk with us unless we paid them. After some debate among us about the ethics of offering an incentive for study participation, we decided to move forward with the plan to offer inmates a small amount of money for speaking with us (see Singer and Bossarte 2006). It is important to take note of the fact that the $5.00 incentive, though small, represented a relatively large amount of money to the inmates who earned only about $0.85 per day. However, there were some interviewees who said that they would have talked with us without the $5.00 payment. Some even told us that they did not want the money because it would be worth their time if the study could help others avoid becoming entangled with guns and convicted of a gun felony. Because correctional policy did not allow us to give the money directly to an inmate, we deposited the funds into each inmate's account when we arrived at the prison prior to the interviews. Thus, incentive payments were made regardless of the quality of the interview and even whether the inmate actually participated in the study.

Of the 119 inmates selected for the study, 73 were available and able to be interviewed. This represents a respectable response rate of 61 percent. In terms of demographics, the overall sample was composed of 39.7 percent whites, 39.7 percent African Americans, 16.4 percent Hispanics, and 4.1 percent Asians and Middle Easterners. Consistent with Colorado statistics on violent crime, 8 percent of the sample were female. Table A1 displays the demographics of inmates incarcerated in Colorado prisons and those interviewed for this study. As Table A1 suggests, the inmates in this sample were considerably more violent than inmates in general. For example, we had no property crime offenders in the sample, even though they make up approximately half of all incarcerated individuals in Colorado's prisons. In addition, the inmate interviewees tended to be somewhat younger than the average Colorado inmate (32.9 years versus 35 years). In fact, nearly half of all the inmates we talked with were between the ages of 20 and 29 years. In comparison, 20- to 29-year-olds make up approximately one-third of Colorado's general prison population. Finally, this sample consists of a greater proportion of African Americans than the general prison population (39.7 versus 22.4). Again, these differences were likely due to the fact that we selected participants based on the nature of their criminal behavior.

Table A1   Comparison of Sample of Gun Offenders to General
            Prison Population, by Selected Characteristics, 2003

	General Prison Population	Entire Sample of Gun Offenders ($n = 73$)
Race/ethnicity		
White	45.8	39.7
Hispanic	28.7	16.4
African American	22.4	39.7
Other	3.1	4.1
Age		
15–19	1.1	1.4
20–29	33.7	49.3
30–39	33.0	26.0
40–49	23.5	8.2
50–59	6.9	11.0
60+	1.9	4.1
Average age (yrs.)	35.0	32.9
Most serious conviction		
Homicide	9.5	39.7
Robbery	6.4	23.3
Kidnapping	1.8	4.1
Assault	8.1	15.1
Sex assault	6.0	0.0
Child sex assault	5.2	0.0
Property crime	48.5	0.0
Habitual	3.1	0.0
Other	11.4	17.8
Sex		
Male	91.8	91.8
Female	8.2	8.2

Response Bias

Response bias is always a concern when a portion of the sample did
not participate. An undetermined number of those not interviewed
had been in administrative segregation, transferred to other prisons,
paroled or otherwise released, or advised by their attorney not to talk
with us due to pending litigation. And lastly, a small number of
selected inmates changed their mind and refused to be interviewed. If
a sample of participants and nonparticipants differs, then the data

131

cannot be used for purposes of generalization. We wanted to determine whether participants ($n = 73$) and nonparticipants ($n = 46$) differed by known characteristics. To examine these differences, we used the logistic regression presented in Table A2. The dependent variable in the logistic regression was whether or not the inmate agreed to be interviewed (i.e., coded as 1 if the inmate agreed to be interviewed and 0 if the inmate did not agree to be interviewed). That dependent variable was then regressed on several potential independent predictors that were known and available in the inmate's prison file. Our finding of no statistically significant differences was desirable, and indicates that response bias was not likely a problem for this analysis. Few differences existed between the two groups. Thus, the inmates interviewed do not appear to be dissimilar from those not interviewed in terms of age, race, sex, sentence length, number of previous felony arrests, and type of crime for which they were incarcerated. Except as described below, inmates who agreed to be interviewed were nearly identical to inmates who did not agree to participate in this study.

As Table A2 indicates, there were two notable differences

Table A2 Logistic Regression Predicting Inmate Participation in Study

Variable	b (SE)
Age (yrs.)	−0.018 (0.027)
Race (vs. white)	
Black	−0.335 (0.491)
Hispanic	0.069 (0.623)
Sex (male = 1)	−1.019 (1.250)
Highest grade completed (yrs.)	0.352 (0.167)*
Married or common law married (yes = 1)	1.108 (0.550)*
Current sentence (yrs.)	0.029 (0.014)
Number of previous felony arrests	−0.093 (0.100)
Previous prison experience (yes = 1)	0.042 (0.508)
Crime (vs. assault and other)	
Murder	0.228 (0.560)
Robbery	0.930 (0.701)
R^2	.19
Log likelihood	−133.71
N	119

*$p < .05$

between participants and nonparticipants. These differences were for the variables of marital status and level of education. In the case of education, the results were not substantively significant and the differences were minor. Each additional year of schooling increased the odds that an offender would participate in the study by a factor of 1.4. On closer inspection, it appears that this effect was entirely due to two particular inmates who agreed to be interviewed. These two inmates had some graduate education, and represented the highest level of education among the 119 inmates randomly selected for interviews. When those two inmates are removed from the sample, the effect of education on study participation completely disappears, which suggests that the effect is largely the result of the combination of a relatively rare event (because graduate degrees among inmates are unlikely) and a small sample.

In the case of marital status, the two groups of inmates—those who participated and those who did not participate—also appear to be different. Married inmates were three times more likely to agree to be interviewed when compared to unmarried inmates. There is no theoretical basis for why this might have been the case, although it is certainly possible that married inmates are more social and therefore looking for contact with the outside world. This finding highlights the possibility that the more social inmates agreed to be interviewed. One response bias question that we cannot address has to do with inmates' perceptions of our role. If we were viewed more as authority figures than as researchers—just through the associations we had with the prison staff as gatekeepers to the inmates—then we believe this could impair the generalizability of our research. Anecdotally, one inmate told us that he had read an article that one of us had previously coauthored (West-Smith, Pogrebin, and Poole 2000) on reasons underlying negative parole decisions. As a result, he told other prisoners that we were trustworthy (or "you're alright" to use his words), thus helping to increase study participation in that prison. In the end, however, information in Tables A1 and A2 does provide us with some comforting evidence that this study is fairly representative of all inmates convicted of gun-related violence in the state of Colorado.

Shall-Issue Concealed Carry Study Subsample

We began our interviews a few months after the Colorado legislature passed and then-governor Bill Owens signed the bill that liberalized

Colorado's concealed carry law. Initially, we did not think to ask inmates their opinions about this new shall-issue law. Once we began talking about guns with inmates, however, we became aware of the importance of this issue when several interviewees brought it up on their own. At that point, we investigated the history and substance of Colorado's shall-issue law and decided to ask all subsequent interviewees about their opinion of the law if they did not already mention it during the course of the discussion. The following example shows how an interviewer asked this question if an inmate did not bring it up on his or her own.

> INTERVIEWER: You've heard about that new concealed weapon law that the Colorado legislature passed?
> INTERVIEWEE: Yes. I've heard about that.
> INTERVIEWER: What do you think about it?

We then listened to answers that the inmates gave regarding their opinions of the shall-issue law and probed them for further explanations as needed (e.g., "Why do you think so?" "Why does carrying a concealed gun increase your feeling of protection?" "How is the new law going to increase/reduce crime?").

The inquiries on the concealed carry law yielded a total of 40 usable responses. The demographics of our subsample were fairly representative of the total sample of inmates in terms of age, race, and sex. However, we found that the gun policy subsample overrepresented inmates convicted of homicide and underrepresented inmates convicted of robbery. Given these differences, and the circumstances under which questions on the concealed carry law came to be an important issue for us to investigate, we do not claim that the final sample of inmates is representative of all prison inmates in Colorado. Yet as noted in Table A3, the concealed carry sample of 40 inmates is remarkably similar to the 73 inmates that we interviewed for the entire study.

Gang Study Subsample

According to our research of their prison files, 24 inmates had been gang members prior to their incarceration. After talking with those inmates, we discovered that they did indeed appear to be gang mem-

Table A3   Comparison of Entire Sample of Gun Offenders and
            Policy Subsample of Offenders, by Selected
            Characteristics

	Entire Sample of Gun Offenders (n = 73)	Subsample of Respondents/ Gun Offenders (n = 40)
Race/ethnicity		
White	39.7	37.5
Hispanic	16.4	20.0
African American	39.7	40.0
Other	4.1	2.5
Age		
15–19	1.4	0.0
20–29	49.3	55.0
30–39	26.0	17.5
40–49	8.2	15.0
50–59	11.0	7.5
60+	4.1	5.0
Average age (yrs.)	32.9	32.8
Most serious conviction		
Homicide	39.7	47.5
Robbery	23.3	15.0
Kidnapping	4.1	00.0
Assault	15.1	15.0
Other	17.8	22.5
Sex		
Male	91.8	90.0
Female	8.2	10.0

bers. Chapter 3 focuses on the gang subsample of gun users. Inmates who had been gang members were asked generally about their families, schools, peer groups, neighborhood, prior contact with the criminal justice system, and experiences with firearms. Their answers, however, were different from the answers given to us by nongang members. Gang socialization as well as views about self and identity began to emerge as important aspects of violence and gun use.

References

Adler, Freda. 1983. *Nations Not Obsessed with Crime*. Littleton, CO: Fred B. Rothman.

Anderson, Elijah. 1999. *Code of the Street: Decency, Violence, and the Moral Life of the Inner City*. New York: W. W. Norton.

Anderson, Leon, and Thomas Calhoun. 1992. "Facilitative Aspects of Field Research with Deviant Street Populations." *Sociological Inquiry* 62(4):490–498.

Atchley, Robert C., and Patrick M. McCabe. 1968. "Socialization in Correctional Communities: A Replication." *American Sociological Review* 33(5):774–785.

Athens, Lonnie. 1997. *Violent Criminal Acts and Actors Revisited*. Urbana: University of Illinois Press.

Bem, Daryl J. 1967. "Self-perception: An Alternative Interpretation of Cognitive Dissonance Phenomena." *Psychological Review* 74(1):183–200.

———. 1972. "Self-perception Theory." In L. Berkowitz (ed.), *Advances in Experimental Social Psychology*. Volume 6. New York: Academic Press, pp. 1–62.

Baumeister, Roy, and Dianne Tice. 1984. "Role of Self-presentation and Choice in Cognitive Dissonance Under Forced Compliance." *Journal of Personality and Social Psychology* 46(1):5–13.

Berger, Peter. 1963. *Invitation to Sociology: A Humanistic Perspective*. Garden City, NY: Doubleday.

Bjerregaard, Beth, and Alan Lizotte. 1995. "Gun Ownership and Gang Membership." *Journal of Criminal Law and Criminology* 86(1):37–58.

Blomberg, Thomas, and Karol Lucken. 2000. *American Penology: A History of Control*. Hawthorne, NY: Aldine de Gruyter.

Blumstein, Alfred. 1995a. "Violence by Young People: Why the Deadly Nexus?" *National Institute of Justice Journal*, no. 229:2–9.

———. 1995b. "Youth Violence, Guns, and the Illicit-Drug Industry." *Journal of Criminal Law and Criminology* 86(1):10–36.

Bottoms, Anthony E. 1999. "Interpersonal Violence and Social Order in Prisons." In M. Tonry and J. Petersilia (eds.), *Crime and Justice: A Review of Research*. Volume 26. Chicago: University of Chicago Press, pp. 205–281.

Bowker, Lee, and Malcolm Klein. 1983. "The Etiology of Female Juvenile Delinquency and Gang Membership: A Test of Psychological and Social Structural Explanations." *Adolescence* 18(6):739–751.

Braga, Anthony A., Glenn L. Pierce, Jack McDevitt, Brenda J. Bond, and Shea Cronin. 2008. "Strategic Prevention of Gun Violence Among Gang-Involved Offenders." *Justice Quarterly* 25(1):132–162.

Broadhead, Robert S., and Ray C. Rist. 1976. "Gatekeepers and the Social Control of Social Research." *Social Problems* 23(3):325–336.

Brody, David, James Acker, and Wayne Logan. 2001. *Criminal Law*. Gaithersburg, MD: Aspen.

Brownstein, Henry H. 2000. *The Social Reality of Violence and Violent Crime*. Boston: Allyn and Bacon.

Bryman, Alan, and Robert G. Burgess. 1994. *Analyzing Qualitative Data*. London: Sage.

Burns, Robert B. 2000. *Introduction to Research Methods*. London: Sage.

Callero, Peter. 1985. "Role Identity Salience." *Social Psychology Quarterly* 48(3):203–215.

Chase, Susan E. 1995. *Ambiguous Empowerment: The Work Narrative of Women School Superintendents*. Amherst: University of Massachusetts Press.

Clemmer, Donald. 1940. *The Prison Community*. Boston: Christopher.

Collins, Randall. 2008. *Violence: A Micro-Sociological Theory*. Princeton: Princeton University Press.

Colorado Department of Corrections. 2004. *Statistical Report, Fiscal Year 2003*. Colorado Springs: Colorado Department of Corrections, Office of Planning and Analysis.

———. 2007. *Statistical Report, Fiscal Year 2006*. Colorado Springs: Colorado Department of Corrections, Office of Planning and Analysis.

Cook, Philip J., and Jens Ludwig, 2000. *Gun Violence: The Real Costs*. New York: Oxford University Press.

Cooke, Claire A. 2004. "Young People's Attitudes Towards Guns in America, Great Britain, and Western Australia." *Aggressive Behavior* 30(1):93–104.

Covey, Herbert C. 2007. *The Methamphetamine Crisis: Strategies to Save Addicts, Families and Communities*. Westport, CT: Praeger.

Daly, Kathleen, and Meda Chesney-Lind. 1988. "Feminism and Criminology." *Justice Quarterly* 5(4):497–535.

Decker, Scott, and Barrik Van Winkle. 1996. *Life in the Gang: Family, Friends, and Violence*. New York: Cambridge University Press.

Denzin, Norman K., and Yvonna S. Lincoln. 1998. *Collecting and Interpreting Qualitative Materials.* Thousand Oaks, CA: Sage.

Dhami, Mandeep, Peter Ayton, and George Loewenstein. 2007. "Adaptation to Imprisonment: Indigenous or Imported?" *Criminal Justice and Behavior* 34(8):1085–1100.

Diener, Edward, and Kenneth W. Kerber. 1979. "Personality Characteristics of American Gun-Owners." *Journal of Social Psychology* 107(2):227–238.

Dunworth, Terence. 2000. *National Evaluation of Youth Firearms Violence Initiative.* Research in Brief. Washington, DC: US Department of Justice, Office of Justice Programs, National Institute of Justice.

Evans, Rhonda D., and Dianne A. Porche. 2005. "The Nature and Frequency of Medicare/Medicaid Fraud and Neutralization Techniques Among Speech, Occupational, and Physical Therapists." *Deviant Behavior* 26(3):253–270.

Fontana, Andrea, and James H. Frey. 1994. "Interviewing: The Art of Science." In N. Denzin and Y. Lincoln (eds.), *Handbook of Qualitative Research.* London: Sage, pp. 361–377.

Fontdevila, Jorge, Nabila El-Bassel, and Louisa Gilbert. 2005. "Accounting for HIV Risk Among Men on Methadone." *Sex Roles* 52(9–10):609–624.

Garfinkel, Harold. 1956. "Conditions of Successful Degradation Ceremonies." *American Journal of Sociology* 61(5):420–424.

Geiger, Brenda, and Michael Fischer. 2003. "Female Repeat Offenders Negotiating Identity." *International Journal of Offender Therapy and Comparative Criminology* 47(5):496–515.

Gendreau, Paul, and David Keyes. 2001. "Making Prisons Safer and More Human Environments." *Canadian Journal of Criminology* 43(1):123–130.

Gerrard, Nathan. 1964. "The Core Member of the Gang." *British Journal of Criminology* 4(3):361–371.

Gillespie, Wayne. 2003. *Prisonization: Individual and Institutional Factors Affecting Inmate Conduct.* New York: LFB Scholarly Publishing.

Gilmore, Ruth W. 2006. *Golden Gulag: Prisons, Surplus, Crisis, and Opposition in Globalizing California.* Berkeley: University of California Press.

Glaser, Barney G., and Anselm L. Strauss. 1967. *The Discovery of Grounded Theory: Strategies for Qualitative Research.* Chicago: Aldine.

Goffman, Erving. 1959. *The Presentation of Self in Everyday Life.* Garden City, NY: Doubleday.

———. 1961a. *Encounters: Two Studies in the Sociology of Interaction.* Indianapolis: Bobbs-Merrill.

———. 1961b. *Asylums: Essays on the Social Situation of Mental Patients and Other Inmates.* Garden City, NY: Doubleday.

———. 1963. *Stigma.* Englewood Cliffs, NJ: Prentice Hall.

———. 1967. *Interaction Ritual: Essays on Face-to-Face Behavior.* Chicago: Aldine.

———. 1974. *Frame Analysis: An Essay on the Organization of Experience.* New York: Harper and Row.

Gordon, Rachel, Benjamin Lahey, Kriko Kawai, Rolf Loeber, Magda Stouthamer-Loeber, and David Farrington. 2004. "Antisocial Behavior and Youth Gang Membership: Selection and Socialization." *Criminology* 42(1):55–88.

Gross, Edward, and Gregory P. Stone. 1964. "Embarrassment and the Analysis of Role Requirements." *American Journal of Sociology* 70(1):1–15.

Gurr, Ted Robert. 1989. *Violence in America: The History of Crime.* Thousand Oaks, CA: Sage.

Hagedorn, John, and Mike Davis. 2008. *A World of Gangs: Armed Young Men and Gangsta Culture.* Minneapolis: University of Minnesota Press.

Harer, Miles D., and Neal P. Langan. 2001. "Gender Differences in Predictors of Prison Violence: Assessing the Predictive Validity of a Risk Classification System." *Crime and Delinquency* 47(4):513–536.

Harlow, Caroline W. 2001. *Survey of Inmates in State and Federal Correctional Facilities: Firearm Use by Offenders.* Washington, DC: US Department of Justice, Bureau of Justice Statistics.

Hemenway, David, Deborah Azrael, and Matthew Miller. 2001. "National Attitudes Concerning Gun Carrying in the United States." *Injury Prevention* 7(4):282–285.

Hepburn, L., Matthew Miller, Deborah Azrael, and David Hemenway. 2007. "The Gun Stock: Results from the 2004 National Firearms Survey." *Injury Prevention* 13(1):15–19.

Hess-Biber, Sharlene, and Patricia Leavy. 2008. *Handbook of Emergent Methods.* New York: Guilford Press.

Hewitt, John P. 1988. *Self and Society.* Boston: Allyn and Bacon.

Hewitt, John P., and Randall Stokes. 1975. "Disclaimers." *American Sociological Review* 40(1):1–11.

Hickman, C. Addison, and Manford Kuhn. 1956. *Individuals, Groups, and Economic Behavior.* New York: Dryden.

Hirschi, Travis, and Michael R. Gottfredson. 1990. *A General Theory of Crime.* Stanford: Stanford University Press.

Hobbs, Dick, and Tim May. 1993. "Foreword." In D. Hobbs and T. May (eds.), *Interpreting the Field: Accounts of Ethnography.* New York: Oxford University Press, pp. vi–xviii.

Holstein, James, and Jaber Gubrium. 2003. *Inner Lives and Social Worlds.* New York: Oxford University Press.

Horowitz, Ruth. 1983. *Honor and the American Dream.* New Brunswick, NJ: Rutgers University Press.

Howell, James. 1998. "Youth Gangs: An Overview." *Juvenile Justice Bulletin* (August). Washington, DC: US Department of Justice, Office of Juvenile Justice and Delinquency Prevention.

Hughes, Lorine, and James Short. 2005. "Disputes Involving Youth Street Gang Members: Micro-Social Contexts." *Criminology* 43(1):43–76.

Ireland, Jane L. 2002. *Bullying Among Prisoners: Evidence, Research and Intervention Strategies.* New York: Brunner-Routledge.

Irwin, John. 1970. *The Felon.* Englewood Cliffs, NJ: Prentice Hall.

Irwin, John, and Donald R. Cressey. 1962. "Thieves, Convicts and the Inmate Culture." *Social Problems* 10(2):142–155.

Jacobs, Bruce, and Richard Wright. 2006. *Street Justice: Retaliation in the Criminal Underworld.* New York: Cambridge University Press.

Jacobs, Bruce A., Volkan Topalli, and Richard Wright. 2003. "Carjacking, Street Life, and Offender Motivation." *British Journal of Criminology* 43(6):673–688.

Jacobs, James B. 1974. "Street Gangs Behind Bars." *Social Problems* 21(3):395–409.

Jiang, Shanhe, and Marianne Fisher-Giorlando. 2002. "Inmate Misconduct: A Test of the Deprivation, Importation, and Situational Models." *The Prison Journal* 82(3):335–358.

Jiobu, Robert M., and Timothy J. Curry. 2001. "Lack of Confidence in the Federal Government and the Ownership of Firearms." *Social Science Quarterly* 82(1):77–88.

Johnson, Kevin. 2007. "Police Needing Heavier Weapons; Chiefs Cite Spread of Assault Rifles." *USA Today,* February 20, p. 1A.

Jones, Edward E., and Thane S. Pittman. 1982. "Toward a Theory of Strategic Self-presentation." In J. Suls (ed.), *Psychological Perspectives on the Self.* Volume 1. Hillsdale, NJ: Lawrence Erlbaum, pp. 231–262.

Jones, Richard S., and Thomas J. Schmid. 2000. *Doing Time: Prison Experience and Identity Among First Time Inmates.* Stamford, CT: JAI Press.

Kalnich, David B., and Stan Stojkovic. 1985. "Contraband: The Basis for Legitimate Power in a Prison Social System." *Criminal Justice and Behavior* 12(4):435–451.

Kanter, Rosabeth. 1972. *Commitment and Community: Communes and Utopias in Sociological Perspective.* Cambridge: Harvard University Press.

Katz, Jack. 1988. *Seductions of Crime: Moral and Sensual Attractions in Doing Evil.* New York: Basic Books.

Kennedy, David M., Ann M. Piehl, and Anthony Braga. 1996. *Youth Gun Violence in Boston: Gun Markets, Serious Youth Offenders, and a Use Reduction Strategy.* Research in Brief. Washington, DC: US Department of Justice, Office of Justice Programs, National Institute of Justice.

Kleck, Gary. 1991. *Point Blank: Guns and Violence in America.* New York: Aldine de Gruyter.

———. 1997. *Targeting Guns: Firearms and Their Control.* New York: Aldine de Gruyter.

Kleck, Gary, and Marc Gertz. 1998. "Carrying Guns for Protection: Results from the National Self-defense Survey." *Journal of Research in Crime and Delinquency* 35(2):193–224.

Kleck, Gary, and Jongyeon Y. Tark. 2004. "Resisting Crime: The Effects of Victim Action on the Outcomes of Crimes." *Criminology* 42(4):861–910.

Klein, Malcolm. 1995. *The American Street Gang.* New York: Oxford University Press.

Knowles, Gordon J. 1999. "Male Prison Rape: A Search for Causation and Prevention." *Howard Journal of Criminal Justice* 38(3):267–283.

Kohn, Abigail A. 2004. *Shooters: Myths and Realities of America's Gun Cultures.* New York: Oxford University Press.

Kopel, David. 1996. "The Untold Triumph of Concealed-Carry Permits." *Policy Review* 78(1):9–11.

Kovandzic, Tom V., and Thomas B. Marvell. 2003. "Right-to-Carry Concealed Handguns and Violent Crime: Crime Control Through Decontrol?" *Criminology and Public Policy* 2(3):363–396.

Kubrin, Charis E. 2005. "Gangstas, Thugs, and Hustlas: Identity and the Code of the Street in Rap Music." *Social Problems* 52(3):360–378.

Kuhns, Joseph B. 2005. "The Dynamic Nature of the Drug Use/Serious Violence Relationship: A Multi-causal Approach." *Violence and Victims* 20(4):433–454.

Lane, Roger. 1997. *Murder in America: A History.* Columbus: Ohio State University Press.

Lasley, James R. 1992. "Age, Social Context, and Street Gang Membership: Are 'Youth' Gangs Becoming 'Adult' Gangs?" *Youth and Society* 23(4):434–451.

Lenzen, John C. 1995. "Liberalizing the Concealed Carry of Handguns by Qualified Civilians: The Case for Carry Reform." *Rutgers Law Review* 47(4):1503–1556.

Lindesmith, Alfred, and Anselm Strauss. 1968. *Social Psychology.* New York: Holt, Rinehart and Winston.

Lizotte, Alan J., and David J. Bordua. 1980. "Firearm Ownership for Sport and Protection: Two Divergent Models." *American Sociological Review* 45(2):229–244.

Lizotte, Alan J., James Tesoriero, Terence Thornberry, and Marvin Krohn. 1994. "Patterns of Adolescent Firearms Ownership and Use." *Justice Quarterly* 11(1):51–74.

Lofland, John, and Lyn H. Lofland. 1995. *Analyzing Social Settings: A Guide to Qualitative Observation and Analysis.* Belmont, CA: Wadsworth.

Lott, John R. Jr. 1998. "Do Shall-Issue Laws Save Lives?" *American Journal of Public Health* 88(9):980–982.

———. 2006. "Do More Guns Lead to Less Crime? Yes." In T. J. Hickey (ed.), *Taking Sides: Clashing Views in Crime and Criminology.* Dubuque, IA: McGraw-Hill Contemporary Learning Series, pp. 266–281.

Ludwig, Jens. 1998. "Concealed Gun Carrying Laws and Violent Crime: Evidence from State Panel Data." *International Review of Law and Economics* 18(3):239–254.

Maxwell, Joseph A. 1996. *Qualitative Research Design: An Interactive Approach.* Thousand Oaks, CA: Sage.

McCall, George, and Jerry Simmons. 1966. *Identities and Interactions: An Examination of Human Associations in Everyday Life.* New York: Free Press.

McCorkle, Richard C. 1992. "Personal Precautions to Violence in Prison." *Criminal Justice and Behavior* 29(2):160–173.

McCorkle, Richard, and Terance Miethe. 2002. *Panic: The Social Construction of the Street Gang Problem*. Upper Saddle River, NJ: Prentice Hall.

Memory, John M., Guang Guo, Ken Parker, and Tom Sutton. 1999. "Comparing Disciplinary Infraction Rates of North Carolina Fair Sentencing and Structured Sentencing Inmates: A Natural Experiment." *The Prison Journal* 79(1):45–71.

Migliaccio, Todd A. 2002. "Abused Husbands: A Narrative Analysis." *Journal of Family Issues* 23(1):26–52.

Miller, Jody, and Rod Brunson. 2000. "Gender Dynamics in Youth Gangs: A Comparison of Males' and Females' Accounts." *Justice Quarterly* 17(3):419–448.

Miller, Jody, and Scott Decker. 2001. "Young Women and Gang Violence: Gender, Street Offender, and Violent Victimization in Gangs." *Justice Quarterly* 18(1):115–140.

Mills, C. Wright. 1940. "Situated Actions and Vocabularies of Motive." *American Sociological Review* 5(6):904–913.

Minichiello, Victor, Rosalie Aroni, Eric Timewell, and Loris Alexander. 1995. *In-Depth Interviewing: Principles, Techniques, Analysis*. Melbourne, Australia: Longman.

Monaghan, Lee F. 2002. "Vocabularies of Motive for Illicit Steroid Use Among Bodybuilders." *Social Science and Medicine* 55(5):695–708.

Moore, Joan. 1978. *Homeboys: Gangs, Drugs, and Prison in the Barrios of Los Angeles*. Philadelphia: Temple University Press.

———. 1991. *Going Down to the Barrio: Homeboys and Homegirls in Change*. Philadelphia: Temple University Press.

Newman, Graeme. 1979. *Understanding Violence*. New York: J. B. Lippincott.

Oliver, William. 1994. *The Violent World of Black Men*. New York: Lexington.

Orbuch, Terri L. 1997. "People's Accounts Count: The Sociology of Accounts." *Annual Review of Sociology* 23(3):455–478.

Pershing, Jana L. 2003. "To Snitch or Not to Snitch? Applying the Concept of Neutralization Techniques to the Enforcement of Occupational Misconduct." *Sociological Perspectives* 46(2):149–178.

Piehl, Ann M., David M. Kennedy, and Anthony Braga. 2000. "Problem Solving and Youth Violence: An Evaluation of the Boston Gun Project." *American Law and Economics Review* 2(1):58–106.

Pierce, Jennifer L. 2003. "Introduction to Special Issue." *Qualitative Sociology* 26(3):307–312.

Pogrebin, Mark. 2003. "Preface." In M. Pogrebin (ed.), *Qualitative Approaches to Criminal Justice*. Thousand Oaks, CA: Sage, pp. xi–xvi.

Presser, Lois. 2004. "Violent Offenders, Moral Selves: Constructing Identities and Accounts in the Research Interview." *Social Problems* 51(1):82–101.

143

Prus, Robert C. 1975. "Resisting Designations: An Extension of Attribution Theory into a Negotiated Conflict." *Sociological Inquiry* 45(1):3–14.

Ross, Jeffrey I., and Stephen C. Richards. 2003. "Introduction: What Is the New School of Convict Criminology?" In J. I. Ross and S. C. Richards (eds.), *Convict Criminology*. Belmont, CA: Wadsworth. pp. 1–12.

Sampson, Robert J., and John H. Laub. 1993. *Crime in the Making: Pathways and Turning Points Through Life*. Cambridge: Harvard University Press.

Sanders, William. 1994. *Gang-Bangs and Drive-bys: Grounded Culture and Juvenile Gang Violence*. New York: Walter de Gruyter.

Schatzman, Leonard, and Anselm Strauss. 1973. *Field Research: Strategies for a Natural Sociology*. Englewood Cliffs, NJ: Prentice Hall.

Scott, Marvin B., and Stanford M. Lyman. 1968. "Accounts." *American Sociological Review* 33(1):46–61.

Scully, Diana, and Joseph Marolla. 1984. "Convicted Rapists' Vocabulary of Motive: Excuses and Justifications." *Social Problems* 31(5):530–544.

Shapiro, Jeremy P., Rebekah L. Dorman, William M. Burkey, Carolyn J. Welker, and Joseph B. Clough. 1997. "Development and Factor Analysis of a Measure of Youth Attitudes Toward Guns and Violence." *Journal of Clinical Child Psychology* 26(2):311–320.

Shelden, Randall, Sharon Tracy, and William Brown. 2001. *Youth Gangs in American Society*. Belmont, CA: Wadsworth.

Sheley, Joseph, and James Wright. 1995. *In the Line of Fire: Youth, Guns and Violence in America*. New York: Aldine de Gruyter.

Sherif, Muzafer, and Milbourne Wilson. 1953. *Group Relations at the Crossroads*. New York: Harper.

Shibutani, Tomatsu. 1961. *Society and Personality: An Interactionist Approach to Social Psychology*. Englewood Cliffs, NJ: Prentice Hall.

Short, James. 1997. *Poverty, Ethnicity, and Violent Crime*. Boulder: Westview Press.

Short, James, and Fred Strodtbeck. 1965. *Group Processes and Gang Delinquency*. Chicago: University of Chicago Press.

Singer, Eleanor, and Robert M. Bossarte. 2006. "Incentives for Survey Participation: When Are They 'Coercive'?" *American Journal of Preventive Medicine* 31(5):411–418.

Sirpal, Suman K. 1997. "Causes of Gang Participation and Strategies for Prevention in Gang Members' Own Words." *Journal of Gang Research* 4(2):13–22.

Smith, Tom W. 2002. "Public Opinion About Gun Policies." *The Future of Children* 12(2):154–163.

Sommers, Ira, and Deborah Baskin. 2006. "Methamphetamine Use and Violence." *Journal of Drug Issues* 36(1):77–96.

Spergel, Irving, and David G. Curry. 1990. "Strategies and Perceived Agency Effectiveness in Dealing with the Youth Gang Problem." In R. C. Huff (ed.), *Gangs in America*. Newbury Park, CA: Sage, pp. 288–309.

Stone, Gregory. 1962. "Appearance and Self." In A. Rose (ed.), *Human Behavior and Social Processes*. Boston: Houghton Mifflin, pp. 86–118.

Strauss, Anselm. 1962. "Transformations of Identity." In A. Rose (ed.),

Human Behavior and Social Processes: An Interactional Approach.
Boston: Houghton Mifflin, pp. 63–85.

———. 1969. *Mirrors and Masks: The Search for Identity.* New York: Macmillan.

Stryker, Sheldon, and Richard Serpe. 1982. "Commitment, Identity Salience and Role Behavior." In W. Ikes and E. Knowles (eds.), *Personality, Roles and Social Behavior.* New York: Springer-Verlag, pp. 199–218.

Swigert, Victoria Lynn, and Ronald A. Farrell. 1977. "Normal Homicides and the Law." *American Sociological Review* 42(1):16–32.

Sykes, Gresham M. 1974. *The Society of Captives.* Princeton: Princeton University Press.

Sykes, Gresham M., and David Matza. 1957. "Techniques of Neutralization: A Theory of Delinquency." *American Sociological Review* 22(6):664–670.

Sykes, Gresham M., and Sheldon L. Messinger. 1960. "The Inmate Social System." In R. Cloward (ed.), *Theoretical Studies in the Social Organization of the Prison.* New York: Social Science Research Council, pp. 6–9.

Tedeschi, James T., and Catherine A. Riordan. 1981. "Impression Management and Pro-social Behavior Following Transgression." In J. T. Tedeschi (ed.), *Impression Management Theory and Social Psychological Research.* New York: Academic Press, pp. 223–244.

Theodoulou, Stella Z., and Chris Kofinis. 2004. *The Art of the Game: Understanding American Public Policy Making.* Belmont, CA: Wadsworth.

Thornberry, Terence, Marvin Krohn, Alan Lizotte, and Debra Chard-Wierschem. 1993. "The Role of Juvenile Gangs in Facilitating Delinquent Behavior." *Journal of Research in Crime and Delinquency* 30(1):55–87.

Thornberry, Terence, Marvin Krohn, Alan Lizotte, Carolyn Smith, and Kimberly Tobin. 2003. *Gangs and Delinquency in Developmental Perspective.* Cambridge: Cambridge University Press.

Thrasher, Frederick. 1927. *The Gang.* Chicago: University of Chicago Press.

Tromanhauser, Edward. 2003. "Comments and Reflections on Forty Years in the American Criminal Justice System." In J. I. Ross and S. C. Richards (eds.), *Convict Criminology.* Belmont, CA: Wadsworth, pp. 81–93.

Tucker, Donald. 1982. "A Punk's Song: View from the Inside." In A. M. Sacco (ed.), *Male Rape: A Case Book of Sexual Aggressions.* New York: AMS Press, pp. 58–79.

Turgeman-Goldschmidt, Orly. 2005. "Hackers' Accounts: Hacking as a Social Entertainment." *Social Science Computer Review* 23(1):8–23.

Turner, Ralph. 1978. "The Role and the Person." *American Journal of Sociology* 84(1):1–23.

Unnithan, N. Prabha. 1986. "Research in a Correctional Setting: Constraints and Biases." *Journal of Criminal Justice* 14(5):401–412.

Utter, Glenn H. 2000. *Encyclopedia of Gun Control and Gun Rights.* Phoenix: Oryx Press.

Vigil, James D. 1988. *Barrio Gangs.* Austin: University of Texas Press.

145

———. 1996. "Street Baptism: Chicago Gang Initiation." *Human Organization* 55(2):149–153.

———. 2003. "Urban Violence and Street Gangs." *Annual Review of Anthropology* 32(2):225–242.

Walker, Samuel. 1998. *Sense and Nonsense About Crime and Drugs.* Belmont, CA: Wadsworth.

Walters, Glenn D. 2003. "Changes in Criminal Thinking and Identity in Novice and Experienced Inmates: Prisonization Revisited." *Criminal Justice and Behavior* 30(4):399–421.

Walzer, Susan, and Thomas P. Oles. 2003. "Managing Conflict After Marriage's End: A Qualitative Study of Narratives of Ex-spouses." *Families in Society* 84(2):192–200.

Weber, Max. 1969. *Wirtschaft und gesellschaft.* Trans. H. P. Secher. New York: Greenwood Press.

Weinstein, Eugene A., and Paul Deutschberger. 1963. "Some Dimensions of Altercasting." *Sociometry* 26(4):454–466.

Welch, Michael. 1996. *Corrections: A Critical Approach.* New York: McGraw-Hill.

West-Smith, Mary, Mark Pogrebin, and Eric Poole. 2000. "Denial of Parole: An Inmate Perspective." *Federal Probation* 64(2):3–10.

Wheeler, Stanton. 1961. "Socialization in Correctional Communities." *American Sociological Review* 26(5):697–712.

Wilcox, Pamela, David C. May, and Staci D. Roberts. 2006. "Student Weapon Possession and the 'Fear and Victimization Hypothesis': Unraveling the Temporal Order." *Justice Quarterly* 23(4):502–529.

Willott, Sara, Christine Griffin, and Mark Torrance. 2001. "Snakes and Ladders: Upper-Middle Class Male Offenders Talk About Economic Crime." *Criminology* 39(2):441–466.

Wilson, Harry L. 2006. *Guns, Gun Control and Elections: The Politics and Policy of Firearms.* Lanham, MD: Rowman and Littlefield.

Winterdyk, John Albert, and Liqun Cao (eds.). 2004. *Lessons from International/Comparative Criminology/Criminal Justice.* Willowdale, Ontario: DaSitter.

Wood, Julia T. 2004. "Monsters and Victims: Male Felons' Accounts of Intimate Partner Violence." *Journal of Social and Personal Relationships* 21(5):555–576.

Wright, James D., and Peter H. Rossi. 1986. *Armed and Considered Dangerous: A Survey of Felons and Their Firearms.* New York: Aldine de Gruyter.

———. 1994. *Armed and Considered Dangerous: A Survey of Felons and Their Firearms: Expanded Edition.* New York: Aldine de Gruyter.

Wright, James D., Peter H. Rossi, and Kathleen Daly. 1983. *Under the Gun: Weapons, Crime and Violence in America.* New York: Aldine.

Wright, Richard T., and Scott H. Decker. 1997. *Armed Robbers in Action: Stickups and Street Culture.* Boston: Northeastern University Press.

Yablonsky, Lewis. 1962. *The Violent Gang.* New York: Macmillan.

Zavitz, Marianne W. 1996. *Firearms, Crime and Criminal Justice: Firearm Injury from Crime.* Washington, DC: Bureau of Justice Statistics.

Index

Accident excuse, 42–43

Accounts: complexity of, 45–47; convincing others and one's self through, 49; and etiology of crime, 24–26; excuses, 19, 26, 38–47, 48*tab*; in explanations of violence, 23; as form of impression management, 25; as "front" to minimize threat to identity, 49; judged for authenticity, 25; justifications, 27–38, 40, 43, 45–47, 49*tab*; and lessening of moral responsibility, 24; little to do with motives at time of event, 50; as management technique, 49; required dissimulation of, 50

Antwan (interviewed inmate), 15*tab*, 33, 80, 81, 99

Appeal to higher loyalties justification, 34–36

Assault, 13, 14*tab*, 15*tab*, 59, 76, 85, 111

Beau (interviewed inmate), 17*tab*, 78

Bob (interviewed inmate), 14*tab*, 115

Boston Gun Project, 73

Brandee (interviewed inmate), 17*tab*, 40, 41

Carlo (interviewed inmate), 17*tab*, 107

Chance (interviewed inmate), 15*tab*, 77, 78, 79, 97, 98

Charlie (interviewed inmate), 15*tab*, 65

Claude (interviewed inmate), 14*tab*, 61, 64, 67, 68, 69, 83, 84, 96, 109

Condemnation of condemners justification, 36

Crime committed: assault, 14*tab*, 15*tab*, 16*tab*, 17*tab*, 59, 76, 85, 111; drug dealing, 58; kidnapping, 14*tab*, 15*tab*, 17*tab*; manslaughter, 96; murder, 14*tab*, 15*tab*, 16*tab*, 17*tab*, 28, 34, 38, 39, 44, 45, 62, 64, 65, 77, 80, 83, 86, 91, 92, 107, 111, 113, 114, 115, 116; robbery, 14*tab*, 15*tab*, 16*tab*, 17*tab*, 30, 34, 40, 41, 69, 84, 90, 107, 111

Culture, gang: attachment of meaning to guns in, xi; centrality of

About the Book

HOW ARE GUNS USED AND VIEWED BY CRIMINALS? DO THESE
views change when they are imprisoned? Where do criminals
obtain guns? And how do laws make firearms more or less accessi
ble? Confronting these contentious questions, *Guns, Violence, and
Criminal Behavior* offers a comprehensive exploration of the social
processes surrounding illegal firearm use and criminal behavior.

The authors draw on in-depth interviews with felons convicted of
gun-related crimes and previous quantitative studies to offer a fresh
look at the key issues of gun violence. Highlighting the overlooked
symbolic influence of guns in criminal situations, their findings under-
score the power of social and cultural forces in affecting gun use.

Mark R. Pogrebin is professor of criminology and criminal justice
in the School of Public Affairs at the University of Colorado–Denver.
His most recent book is *About Criminals: A View of the Offender's
World.* **Paul B. Stretesky** is associate professor of criminology and
criminal justice in the School of Public Affairs at the University of
Colorado–Denver. He coauthored *Environmental Law, Crime, and
Justice.* **N. Prabha Unnithan** is professor of sociology and director
of the Center for the Study of Crime and Justice at Colorado State
University. He is editor of the *Social Science Journal.* He coauthored
*Currents of Lethal Violence: An Integrated Model of Suicide and
Homicide.*